Fierce
Teaching

Fierce Teaching

Purpose, Passion,

and

What Matters Most

ERIC JENSEN

CORWIN
PRESS
A SAGE Company

Copyright © 2009 by Corwin Press

For information:

Corwin Press
A SAGE Company
2455 Teller Road
Thousand Oaks, California 91320
www.corwinpress.com

SAGE India Pvt. Ltd.
B 1/I 1 Mohan Cooperative
 Industrial Area
Mathura Road, New Delhi 110 044
India

SAGE Ltd.
1 Oliver's Yard
55 City Road
London EC1Y 1SP
United Kingdom

SAGE Asia-Pacific Pte. Ltd.
33 Pekin Street #02-01
Far East Square
Singapore 048763

Printed in the United States of America.

Library of Congress Cataloging-in-Publication Data

Jensen, Eric, 1950-
Fierce teaching : purpose, passion, and what matters most / Eric Jensen.
    p. cm.
Includes bibliographical references and index.
ISBN 978–1–4129–6329–9 (cloth)
ISBN 978–1–4129–6330–5 (pbk.)
    1. Teaching. 2. Effective teaching. 3. Learning, Psychology of. I. Title.

LB1025.3.J458 2009
371.102—dc22   2008011273

This book is printed on acid-free paper.

08   09   10   11   12   10   9   8   7   6   5   4   3   2   1

Acquisitions Editors:	Allyson P. Sharp, Carol Chambers Collins
Editorial Assistants:	David Andrew Gray, Brett Ory
Production Editor:	Cassandra Margaret Seibel
Copy Editor:	Sarah J. Duffy
Typesetter:	C&M Digitals (P) Ltd.
Proofreader:	Kevin Gleason
Indexer:	Sheila Bodell
Cover Designer:	Rose Storey

Contents

Preface

I didn't always love school, but I've always loved learning. It is truly one of the great joys in life: the moment of discovery, the satisfaction of understanding, and the pride in having learned new things. That love of learning has been the fuel for my professional life for well over 30 years. It's also what brought me back to do this work. It's what I value so highly: learning.

The theme of this book is simple: If you want educators to succeed, help them understand and use the core principles and strategies that drive learning. Then support their efforts to make the changes. That's it. This is not nanotechnology, it's not brain surgery, and it's certainly not like building a space shuttle. It's straightforward. Most educators want their students to succeed and to become contributing members of society. That's why they got into their jobs to begin with. Most educators love to learn, and most enjoy helping others succeed at learning.

But what principles actually govern the success of students at school? We can isolate factors, but schools are classic models of complexity. Very little research explores the underlying fundamentals of such a question. So why would I write a book on this topic? The answer is that a great deal can be learned, but only if you're willing, as a reader, to think a bit differently.

First, let's start with the book's title. The word *fierce* can evoke images of swashbuckling pirates, evil armies, martial artists, or villains. In the context of teaching, it takes on a different, more manageable meaning. *Fierce teaching* means an unrelenting, focused truth. Take it with a sense of purpose, discipline, and action.

Fierce teaching is the process of learning to do what matters most. Just as important, it is learning to *not* do what is irrelevant. Becoming ensconced in an educational trend once is no problem. However, over the years, most teachers have added so many strategies to their arsenal of teaching that they forget the original significance (if any) of each one. It doesn't have to be that way.

Sometimes what's hot in education is not necessarily new. In fact, this book is not about what's hot, trendy, or this year's buzzword; it's about what's important. If you believe that learning and student empowerment are important, then this book is for you. And if improving learning and transforming lives are important to you, you've chosen well.

Second, this book invites you to embrace a whole new way of thinking about learning. The principles that matter are those that frame this book. Not statistical averages, not insignificant correlations, and not multiple regressions, but make-or-break principles. Every one of the key principles in this book matters enough that it can make the difference between a student learning or not learning. When you do enough of the right things, but not too much, you often get a new experience called *fierce teaching*. What's unique about fierce teaching is that it combines the scholarship of learning (both the process and the content) with the commitments to take action. The empowerment comes from seeing ourselves as people who can transform ourselves by transforming others.

Schools have the mandate to foster development of learner assets and capacities that can make for a more positive community and, eventually, the planet. I advocate schools that are committed to making a difference in the lives of students, not schools that operate from fear. Schools have the responsibility to design and facilitate change in individuals, groups, organizations, and cultures. In this process of intentional growth, the learners themselves are changed. By the way, when student assets go up and students are empowered, test scores go up as a by-product. That's the power of transformation; it does more than what you bargained for, not less.

Finally, how do we see our schools and communities as facilities for growth instead of ones that play the testing game? We all know schools aren't perfect. But they don't need to be perfect, and neither do their staff. Schools need to do enough things right so that the aggregate effect is a net positive. Educators understand that many problems they currently wrestle with are a function of other, deeper, more core problems. In a disrespectful environment, students often disengage in class. When students have a tough time learning, they resort to apathy and outlandish behavior. The fact is that learning solves problems. Visit a school that works, and witness how it serves success to its students. If your school has problems, don't put off the fundamentals of learning—for they are at the core of your success—in order to put in place more security scanners, tighter expulsion policies, and quick-triggered disciplinarians. When learning goes up, problems go down.

When you use the principles in this book, you will discover that schools really are about learning, not the other things that frustrate you every day. Do what matters, and cut out the nonessentials. *Fierce Teaching* is simple: show up, do what matters most, and go home happy. Thousands of teachers already are doing it. You, too, can do it; this book will help you get there.

—Eric Jensen

Acknowledgements

I appreciate the tireless work of Carolyn Pool who provided extraordinary organizational and editing work. I also appreciate the support of the Corwin staff who worked hard to make this work accessible to all teachers. Duke Kelly helped make possible several of the cartoon-like illustrations. The title comes from Susan Scott's brilliant work, which was referred to me by Ernest Izard. Finally, I am most grateful for all of the teachers who continually provide me with feedback on my work.

About the Author

**Eric Jensen** began teaching at the middle school level. He has taught temporary assignments at the elementary and high school levels and served as an adjunct faculty member at three California universities. In 1982, he cofounded SuperCamp, the world's first brain-compatible academic enrichment program for students. That trailblazing program has shown that you can get miracles with students when you focus relentlessly on what works. To date, it has had over 45,000 graduates.

He helped introduce brain-based learning to Australia, Denmark, New Zealand, Singapore, Sweden, Hong Kong, and South Africa. Jensen has authored 24 books on the brain and learning, including the bestselling *Teaching With the Brain in Mind, SuperTeaching, Tools for Engagement,* and *Enriching the Brain.* He has spoken at many national and international conferences, and his work has been featured in *USA Today,* the *Wall Street Journal,* and on CNN.

Considered the leader in the field of brain-based learning, Jensen is a staff developer, conference speaker, and member of the Society for Neuroscience and the New York Academy of Sciences. He is currently completing his PhD in human development. Jensen offers in-depth programs and trainings (www.jensenlearning.com) and may be reached for conference speaking and trainings at diane@jlcbrain.com.

Introduction

WHAT IS FIERCE TEACHING?

Fierce teaching describes a way of working with students that is smart and highly effective; it allows you to teach without burnout. It's laser-like in its methodology. Fierce teaching is about doing the right things and doing them right. It asks you to focus on the fewest moving parts to get the greatest effect possible. This book is not about the myths, the popular topics, and the latest trend. It's about learning the factors that make successful teaching possible, every time. In fact, if anything, this book may astound you in the simplicity of the factors that matter most.

What about better strategies? Strategies make things happen in a classroom. However, some teachers use what seem like good strategies, but fail. And other teachers take a marginal strategy and find a way to make it a success. What causes the difference? One of the reasons that a strategy fails is how a teacher uses it. But I believe, as do a number of other researchers cited in this book, that the reason for the variance lies elsewhere.

Look to a larger context when framing the success of strategies. You will see an environment filled with nuances that emerge from a teacher over time. The student experiences a teacher's mission; purpose; and (more explicitly) his or her beliefs, values, principles, and strategies. Typically, more experienced educators understand these domains better, since they have developed some congruency within them. Over time, integration and congruency of these strategies contribute to their effectiveness because they avoid working at odds with each other. Here is the typical hierarchy that experienced educators work with, starting at the top:

- **Mission** is your lifelong job or path. (e.g., "Make a positive, significant, and lasting difference in how we learn").
- **Purpose** is the reason you work. We all need to earn a living, but this is greater than the paycheck. This is the satisfaction, the "hook" in the job you have (e.g., "To discover and share my gifts").

- **Beliefs** are your decision-making foundations. Each of us may have hundreds and thousands of content- and context-dependent beliefs, which influence our decision making. It's easy to see how these can make or break a teacher (e.g., "I believe all students can improve").
- **Values** are your motivational switches. These are the simple mechanisms that influence you to avoid or embrace an idea or action. These values often make the difference between whether we take action on something (e.g., "I value the love of learning, so I'll make the process enjoyable").
- **Principles** are the guiding laws. Such larger categories hold strategies. For example, if the principle is awareness of the environment, the strategy is to influence the environment as much as possible (e.g., "The brain is highly aware on both conscious and nonconscious levels").
- **Strategies** are the daily work tools. Each principle can generate 5 to 500 strategies. Strategies are often population, content, and context specific (e.g., "Student feedback every 30 minutes or less").

Seven Fierce and Highly Practical Strategies

By necessity, most teachers are highly practical; strategies often have a greater appeal than theories, generalized understandings, or ideas. We can all understand that need. But there is a downside. All strategies have an unlimited number of nuances that can make them succeed or fail. It is often assumed strategies are used the same by all, but this is not true. At issue here is that a really good teacher can make a marginal strategy work, and a marginal teacher can ruin a really good strategy. That's why this book focuses not only on strategies, but also on the deeper, more potent principles that underlie them. If you make a change in a strategy on your own, that's fine as long as you understand the general principle.

How the Seven Principles and Strategies Were Chosen

Collectively, it is hard for educators to vote on the "most important" principles. So how is this book different from others? It's different in that it isn't a guide on how to get the highest possible achievement scores in your state. Rather, here are the questions that form the foundation of this book: What are the fundamental principles of learning that will stand the test of time? Which principles, when used on a daily basis, will consistently create positive, significant, and lasting results? And, just as important, are they supportable by the latest research? In short, the methods behind writing this book are as follows:

- establish criteria for research
- locate all research-supportable achievement factors
- gather source materials
- group items by similarities

- eliminate duplication and repetition
- separate strategies from larger principles
- sort criteria from the principles
- test all principles for validity
- develop a model

So that you have a complete understanding of my selection process, here are the characteristics I required in order for each potential principle to make the final cut:

- improve student learning
- be relatively easy to learn and use by an average teacher
- be easy to customize for differentiation
- have no ethnic, religious, or racial bias
- be strongly supported by basic and/or applied research
- support complex as well as simple learning
- be generalizable to wide audience (K–12, adult learning, special education)
- have the capacity for transformative learning
- be teacher tested and classroom proven
- have clarity and coherence for understanding and communication
- be in alignment with recent brain and cognitive science research
- be a plausible and practical source for generating new strategies
- be so important that if it's not used, learning breaks down

The selection process was quite narrowing, so you might not see your favorite tool, strategy, or principle. But I am able to recommend this list of principles without reservation. To choose the principles, I took a vast number of possible factors and sorted them endlessly until something useful emerged.

Using Fierce Principles and Strategies

As I mentioned earlier, this book is primarily about make-or-break learning principles and strategies. I'm interested in factors that are the difference between a student learning or not learning. I trust that you will be able to read and digest the conclusions in the spirit in which they were intended. That is, I want to both shed light upon certain principles and hopefully encourage a path in that direction.

By the way, some learning is actually very simple. Quick surface learning (e.g., word = definition, state = capital) is *simple learning*. You need little or no help for that. This type of learning is easy and goes on all the time. As we start to focus on *complex learning,* however, let's use this definition:

Complex learning (in the educational context) is contrasted with simple, dead-end, or inert accumulation. Typically, it is the acquisition of new content or skills that must be learned in multiple steps.

It takes both time and attention, and typically requires some background (content and schematic buildup) in the learner. Complex learning requires integration of prior and current knowledge, and most important, it engages the learner in both multilevel analysis and application in ways that may change behaviors.

This definition suggests that a substantial amount of learning in school is actually simple learning. It's the aggregate effects of learning and behavior that count, so don't worry about the ratio of complex to simple right now. Over time, as you apply the principles in this book, you'll see more complex learning. But your goal should not be to have most or all learning at school be complex. Some learning at school needs to be simple. Occasionally, students just need to memorize some basics, such as the teacher's name, a locker number, or the essential facts in a unit. It is simple learning that creates the scaffolding for complex learning. To keep the learning of this book's principles simple, consider the acronym BE FIERCE:

BE—body and emotional connections

F—feedback and error correction

I—input-to-output ratio

E—elaboration for depth

R—recall and memory management

C—content coherence

E—environmental management

The upcoming chapters feature principles and strategies of instruction that are absolutely essential to any and all complex learning. They are the make-or-break elements, meaning that if you remove just one of them, complex learning breaks down. Not occasionally, but every single time. These are not elements that can tweak learning or guarantee it—they are absolutely necessary to even have a chance at it. You cannot gain mastery in teaching until you have mastered the most basic principles of learning. The journey's going to be exciting, so hop aboard.

Strategy 1

Body and Emotional Connections

BODY-MIND EMOTIONAL ENGAGEMENT

In an ideal world, every student would show up with a hungry, insatiable desire to learn and be hopeful for success. Obviously, this doesn't always happen. But students do need to be emotionally engaged in order to master the content. Without some type of support or emotional-state management, students might drift, lose interest, and only conquer simple learning, leaving them behind their classmates. For many students, it's how they feel about learning, the curriculum, their teacher, and their peers that dictates school success.

As a rule, students don't perceive that they have much control over how they feel. The negative states of worry, disengagement, and distress all contribute to lower cognitive performance (Matthews et al., 2002). However, there is a wide body of literature showing that the opposite is also true: positive emotional states help students learn more. *Positive affect* positively has an effect on performance and achievement (Ashby, Isen, & Turken, 1999). Brain research, clinical research, and applied classroom research tell us that when students feel good about themselves and about learning, they will perform better. Consider this: we each have a brain, which, by design and function, allows emotions to have a significant influence over most of our life (Bechara, Damasio, & Damasio, 2003).

Practical Suggestion for Engaging Students

- What can you do to get students in better emotional and psychological states? Begin by learning to recognize their emotional states. Take cues from students' body language in terms of their learning potential. Slumped over and poor posture does not indicate a readiness to learn. If you see this in students, provide them with a stretch break, a walking activity, an energizer, a role-play, or a cooperative activity. Going to school is not a choice for students. There are only two reasons 90 percent of them show up: it's the law and their friends are there. To make it relevant, we must do more than provide content; we must provide an environment that encourages returning each day.

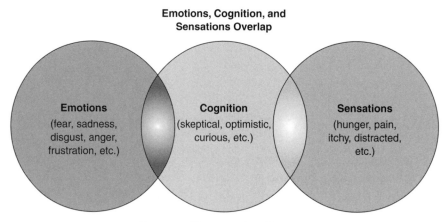

Emotions, Cognition, and
Sensations Overlap

Emotions
(fear, sadness, disgust, anger, frustration, etc.)

Cognition
(skeptical, optimistic, curious, etc.)

Sensations
(hunger, pain, itchy, distracted, etc.)

States combine these 3 and form the
internal environment for learning

Five Key Emotional States

There are five primary emotional states required for complex learning:

1. Safety

2. Vesting

3. Connection

4. Alertness

5. Hope

First and foremost, students must feel safe to learn, safe to take risks, and safe to succeed (even when it's not cool to do so). Second, students must feel vested in the content itself. They need to buy into the subject matter enough to want to work hard at it. Third, they need to feel some kind of emotional connectedness to either the teacher or their classmates. This relationship of belonging will carry many students long past where the potentially lower expectations from their prior teachers or classmates might have taken them. Fourth, they need the mental alertness to pay attention and be focused in class. This alertness provides the working memory, the tuning in, and sharp eyes and ears for complex learning. Finally, students need hope. The magical and always powerful state of hope says, "No matter what today brings, tomorrow might be better." For some, hope is all it takes.

Imagine what kind of experience it would be in your classroom if your students felt safe to learn, to risk, and to make mistakes. Imagine that they felt vested in the content and the process of learning. Imagine that they felt connected and stayed hopeful and alert in class. Does that sound good to you? It is possible—you just have to know how to do it. There are specific strategies that you can use to elicit each of the key emotional states.

Safety

Many schools are so focused on raising achievement scores that they ignore student safety. Often the same teachers who ignore safety comment that students won't focus in class. But emotions and cognition are highly

+   −

Positive States   Negative States
for Learning   for Learning

curiosity   fear
anticipation   anger
"flow" state   distress
confusion   boredom/apathy
"ah-ha!"   worthlessness
concentration   embarrassment

Sample of Student States
When you positively influence student states,
you change their brains temporarily and help
them make positive associations with learning
as well as change their behavior and learning.

related (Gray, Braver, & Raichle, 2002). Students are more violent and fight more than most educators think; more than 1 in 3 kids have been in a fight in the past year, and 1 in 11 have been threatened or injured with a weapon on school property (Ozer, Park, Paul, Brindis, & Irwin, 2003). In addition, more than 4 in 10 male students reported having been in a physical fight during the past month (Kann et al., 2000).

Unequivocal brain research tells us that memory-retrieval processes are usually impaired by high circulating levels of stress hormones (Roozendaal, 2002). The research is clear: when stress goes up, our working memory goes down (Newcomer et al., 1999). We do worse under moderate to significant threat because strong emotions impair cognitive processing (Simpson, Snyder, Gusnard, & Raichle, 2000). When students are under moderate to strong threat, their capacity to do complex thinking is highly impaired.

Increases in stress undermine new memory function (Kim & Diamond, 2002). Classrooms that allow threats, bullying, harassment, and put-downs impair student learning (Wessler, 2004). Increasing security by making your school look like a prison doesn't help performance. Students will pay extra attention to social threats because they are so vulnerable to and concerned with them (van Honk et al., 2000). So if security bars on windows just may lower student achievement scores (Heschong Mahone Group, 2008), what can be done?

Brains Under Threat

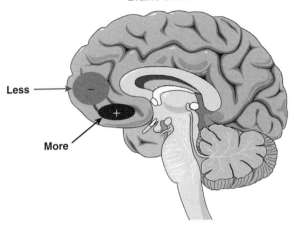

Less

More

Cerebral Blood Flow Changes During Threat

Among the many changes, there is increased ventral prefrontal and decreased dorsal prefrontal activity. This gives us less activation in areas of the brain needed for thinking, creativity, problem-solving and judgment. It increases bloodflow in the area associated with emotional processing, which increases our awareness of the threat.

Practical Suggestions for Creating a Safe Haven

- Start verbalizing respect with the implementation of small acts. Ensure that there are programs or policies in place at your school that reinforce the importance of tolerance of and respect for all. Allow students to air their grievances by using peer counseling and establishing a peer mediation program. Use "please" and "thank you" as well as other polite phrases when conversing with students. Post the seven courtesies that "lubricate" social contact and model them: "Please," "Thank you," "I'm sorry," "I was wrong," "How can I help?" "You're forgiven," and "Can we work this out together?"
- Stamp out bullying. Bullying means that someone is systematically and chronically being hurtful to other students. This can come from teachers who want to "put kids in their place" or from other students. Teachers who bully need to learn alternative strategies that avoid putting kids down. There's no excuse for bullying from staff members. Make sure the staff understands all the various forms of threats. In schools where there is a higher incidence of violence, the tendency is to respond to student violence with more power, more shows of position, and threats. Unfortunately, that response simply exacerbates the problems. Troublesome students don't get better with adult role models who simply bully them back. Staff who bully are undermining the entire school and, in some cases, ruining kids' lives.

Learn to recognize the telltale signs of bullying; kids may not say anything to you. Kids may come home with torn clothes or complain of headaches, stomachaches, or trouble sleeping. The message to all school leaders is, if you want to improve test scores, get the bullying out of your school. Students also can take certain actions to reduce bullying. Tell them what it is so that they recognize it and refuse to hide it or ignore it. Kids who bully often look for kids who are alone, so it's good to walk with buddies at school. If bullying occurs, get it reported and acted upon. You should have a zero-tolerance policy for it. When schools are safe, students can learn. Safety is an absolute prerequisite for all complex learning. To boost achievement, put a schoolwide safety check on your to-do list.

Tips When Working With Parents

- When parents are part of the awareness of the problem, they can become part of the solution, too. Send simple materials home, hold parent nights, and strengthen communications by using Web sites and e-mail.
- Do not make positive school climate an option—get students involved in activities that build character (e.g., scouts, church, 4H, community work).
- Encourage parents to talk often and openly with their children about school and to tell them that they are loved and valued.

Empower students to better handle their own emotions and stressors (McCraty, Atkinson, Tomasino, Goelitz, & Mayrovitz, 1999). Doing so gives you more of a multiplier effect because students affect other students. Give your staff time to work together in small teams, then build consensus with a larger collegial group to develop effective, nonbullying responses to threats. Learn and practice what to say and how to watch your body language (which is often half the threat) and your tonality. Many staff members are simply unaware of how they might be part of the problem.

Vesting

You can bribe students, you can threaten them, but it doesn't change their intrinsic motivation or vesting. The more you artificially try to push students to perform for a big test, the more you run the risk of backfiring. This is called the *paradox of achievement*: the harder you push, the worse it gets (Deci & Ryan, 2002). Pull students in: build assets, help them care, and give them the opportunity to set sails in their own direction. Many studies have shown that goal-driven learning proceeds faster than random learning. Learning enhances the brain's systems, which are continually contrasting output with input and making corrections to the balance of information. As a generalization, greater student vesting in the learning process means better student achievement. This is especially critical at the secondary level, when kids often complain that most or all of their classes are simply boring.

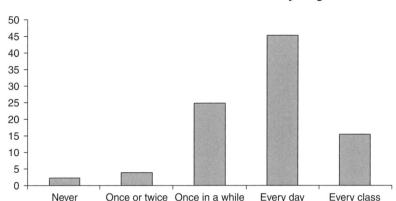

How Often Are Students Bored? 1 in 7 *in Every Single Class*

SOURCE: Yazzie-Mintz, 2007.

Edward Deci and Richard Ryan, at the University of Rochester, have developed a well-regarded self-determination theory (SDT) over the past 30 years, validated by a wide body of research. SDT says that there are three innate psychological needs: (1) competence, "I can do it"; (2) autonomy, "I'm free to do it"; and (3) relatedness, how we feel about each other (Ryan & Deci, 2000). SDT includes the values of emotions, personal efficacy, and choice.

Many factors influence vesting, including students' perception of their own assets. Asset building is essential. At the elementary and secondary levels, studies support this approach. In one study, perceived competence was significantly related to achievement at each school grade in both reading and mathematics (Bouffard, Marcoux, Vezeau, & Bordeleau, 2003). Even in the first grade, there is a strong correlation between academic engagement and perceptions of competence (Valeski & Stipek, 2001). Compared to rewards, developing greater autonomy leads to better-integrated self-regulation. Use emotional intelligence as part of the asset building. Middle school students who are taught emotional self-management skills improve in many areas (McCraty et al., 1999), including the following:

- stress and anger management
- risky behavior
- work management and focus
- relationships with family, peers, and teachers

Practical Suggestions for Developing Greater Vesting

- Recognize the power of affirmations. The more you affirm, the more you get back.
- Thank students for being in class.
- Build safety and make it OK to make mistakes.

(Continued)

(Continued)

- Build students' working assets in study skills, note taking, and memory making.
- Thank students for raising their hands, for *any* contribution.
- Notice when they finish on time.
- Help them set goals and check on completed goals.
- Teach students how to make good choices, and then slowly let them make increasingly more responsible choices.
- Help create connections and relevancy between what students are learning and their own set of values and goals.
- As a better alternative to using rewards, help support students' autonomy (Joussemet, Koestner, Lekes, & Houlfort, 2004). With better vesting, you get more motivated students.

Connection

Positive relationships lower stress, provide role models for learning, and create a climate for performance. In fact, children's reports of relatedness can predict classroom engagement over the course of the school year. Specific relatedness to parents, teachers, and peers makes unique contributions to students' engagement, especially their emotional engagement (Furrer & Skinner, 2003). Students are often timid, arrogant, or self-centered, or they simply lack the confidence or emotional skills to make new acquaintances in school. Yet peer relations have a strong influence on their lives (Gifford-Smith & Brownell, 2003). Having positive social status or being in the right status group strongly correlates with achievement (Marjoribanks, 2003). Don't leave relationships to chance; when you are proactive and create a positive peer climate, you can reduce problems, such as peer aggression, and improve academic focus (Barth, Dunlap, Dane, Lochman, & Wells, 2004).

In a two-year study of more than 300 children, peer rejection assessed as early as kindergarten was stable across the two years and was highly correlated with deficits in first- and second-grade academic achievement and work habits (O'Neil, Welsh, Parke, Wang, & Strand, 1997). Another important study found that interpersonal bonding spreads positive factors for student achievement and behaviors; preventive interventions that result in improved academic performance also lead to moderate improvements in problem behavior (Najaka, Gottfredson, & Wilson, 2001). You can support the development and maintenance of positive affiliations in many ways, including the use of cooperative learning groups, mentoring, competitions, and interest groups.

Practical Suggestions for Developing Connections

- Remember to share brief personal stories about yourself—what you did over the weekend or how you are handling a difficult (but not intense) problem. Students need to connect to you. Also, learn to manage your own emotional states. Take a break for a few seconds to decompress from stress before addressing a student. Otherwise, you might say something you'll regret.

- Learn the skills of framing the content to make it emotionally relevant to students. Relevance is an effective emotion builder (Assor, Kaplan, & Roth, 2002).
- Generate activities in class that elicit emotions. These may include competitions, storytelling, performance arts, journaling, speaking before others, conducting interviews, and telling personal stories. These activities create the emotional binding between student and content, student and teacher, and student and the physical classroom.
- Some groupings, like long-term project teams, are more formal. Students may need team-building activities—and time—to build relationships; don't throw students together and expect that synergy will magically appear.
- Help students learn more about each other as you ask them to form teams or pairs. For example, ask students to go to each of four corners based on which of four movies they think was the best (they have to choose one).
- Once students start feeling more comfortable with each other, you can give more personal prompts, such as "Before we begin, tell your partner one thing about yourself that the other would never know just by looking at you. You get 60 seconds." Always close an activity by saying, "Please thank your partner."

Alertness

You can boost alertness with movement activities. Most types of movement and exercise improve brain levels of dopamine, noradrenaline, and serotonin, all known to enhance mood (Chaouloff, 1989). Plus, these enhanced brain chemicals remain present for a while, and thus support other arousal factors such as memory or alertness (Krock & Hartung, 1992). Remarkably, exercise may even enhance opioid activity (in pleasure and analgesic sites; Sforzo, Seeger, Pert, Pert, & Dotson, 1986). Through games, students can learn or review material in far less threatening conditions than in a formal classroom. The percentages on the left of the graph below are the variations of the baseline. In this case, the baseline is sitting in a chair. Standing up and other active processes increase heart rate and also the amines ("uppers") in the brain such as norepinephrine. That can boosts alertness.

Exercise improves brain function (Tomporowski, 2003) and contributes to specialized and highly important growth factors (Gomez-Pinilla, So, & Kesslak, 1998), which are essential for cognition and brain growth. A study of seventh graders suggests that physical activity may reduce risk for depression and other mood disorders (Motl, Birnbaum, Kubik, & Dishman, 2004). Physical activity may also support improved reading for some students (Reynolds, Nicolson, & Hambly, 2003). Another study found that the social aspect of physical activity creates positive affiliations (A. Smith, 2003). Overall, it is important to include movement breaks several times per hour.

Percent Change in Heart Rate and Norepinephrine: Activity vs. Sitting

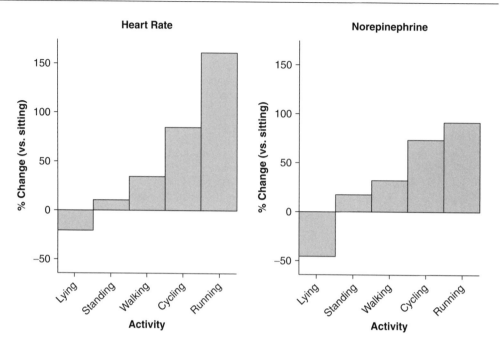

Advantage? Increased circulation means more blood flow and oxygen to the brain. Norepinephrine serves as a memory "fixative" and in moderate amounts will strengthen memories.

SOURCE: Gillberg, Anderzen, Akerstedt, & Sigurdson, 1986.

Practical Suggestions for Adding Alertness to the Classroom

- stand-up breaks
- unusually curious or meaningful work
- teacher-led and/or student-led energizers
- new temporary groups, cooperative learning, and partners
- choosing and identifying novelty identifiers
- use of upbeat, high-tempo music
- games, competition, activities
- a short walk within the classroom
- asking mobilizing, engaging questions

Hope

Hope is the belief that the future will be better. It provides motivation, determination, and persistence. Supporting positive expectancy is important; it's what keeps many kids in school. High-hopeful students are much more likely to receive better overall grade point averages (even after controlling for variance related to entrance examination scores) than

low-hopeful students, and they are more likely to graduate and not have been dismissed (C. Snyder et al., 2002).

Hope does not have to be provable or testable any more than a person's faith in God does. If you lose hope in low-achieving students, you may contribute to their downfall (Zohar & Vaaknin, 2001). On the other hand, as a rule, when students have a positive emotional affect, their achievement increases (Ashby et al., 1999). Hope can be built in many ways—through goals, high expectations, affirmations, success stories, and asset building.

In regard to high expectations, years ago Robert Rosenthal gave an intelligence test to all of the students at the beginning of the school year and randomly selected 20 percent of the students. He told the teachers that these students showed unusual potential for intellectual growth and might "bloom" in academic performance by the end of the year (remember, they were randomly selected). At year's end, he retested all of the students. Those labeled as "intelligent" showed significantly greater increases in the final tests than the other, nonselected children. This suggests that the change in the teachers' intellectual expectations of the children led to an actual change in their performance compared to the randomly selected children. Teachers' negative beliefs about low-achieving students and higher-order thinking hurt student achievement. This understanding of the power of expectancy has been reviewed and verified several times over the years (Rosenthal 1991) and (Rosenthal and Jacobson 1996).

Given that high expectations dramatically influence student perfor- mance, why is creating hope so important? Today's students often have stressful, disjointed lives. In 2001, over one fourth of adolescents ages 14–17 reported episodes of serious depression in the previous 12 months (Centers for Disease Control and Prevention, 2002). About one in seven children and adolescents has an anxiety disorder, and one in five seriously considered suicide in the past 12 months (U.S. Surgeon General, 1999). In 2002, nearly one third of all adolescents ages 12–17 lived with one or no parents (Bryson, 1996; U.S. Census Bureau, 2007). Students need to hear affirmations every day.

Use your influence to plant potentially lifelong positive messages. As an authority figure, you need to declare to students they can and will make it—these are compelling words. Students put up with enough negatives and pessimism in their lives. When you offer a positive, compelling vision of their potential future, it may be all some students need to hear.

Practical Strategies for Helping Students Maintain a Positive Outlook

- Give students time to read positive goals and share successes. Create a climate of "good things happen here." Acknowledge when small goals are reached.
- Overtly and explicitly communicate high expectations to students. These high teacher expectations—what you think of your students' potential—are essential for best performance.
- Keep mental track of the positives-to-negatives ratio. Keep the positives far ahead of the negatives. Be positive when you give directions, talk privately, or call on students in a group.
- Be sure to use role-modeling. When students see and hear you have positive expectancies about the future, it becomes contagious. Share stories about other students who have graduated and succeeded.
- Teach optimism. Read *Learned Optimism* (Seligman, 2006). Focus on strengthening the three pillars of optimism: positive states, engaged life (busy, giving to others), and making meaning of everyday experiences.

SUMMARY

This chapter reviewed the five primary emotional states required for com- plex learning. Students must feel safe—safe to learn, safe to take risks, and safe to succeed. They must feel vested and buy in to the subject matter enough to want to work hard at it. They need an emotional connection to either the teacher or their classmates. They need the alertness and mental acuity to pay attention and be focused. And they need hope. Hope is just as powerful as any other engaged emotional state. It means, "I'll keep try- ing to succeed, even when it seems unlikely I can make it." By themselves, these five critical, engaged states will not guarantee that you'll succeed with your students. But without them, your students have little or no chance. The good news is that you have the capacity to influence those emotional states. No one is telling you that you can control student emotions, but a change in activity, a softer voice, more inclusive class questioning, and dozens of other strategies will bring students into better emotional states. You are not a victim of how students feel when they walk into your room. The fierce teacher makes it a habit and a priority to influence and even manage the emotional states of his or her students.

Strategy 2

Feedback and
Error Correction

THE IMPORTANCE OF FEEDBACK

In choosing the seven most essential strategies for "cut to the chase" teaching, feedback emerges as critical, and with flying colors! Many of us have experienced the disconnect in college courses where the only feedback was on a midterm or final. Feedback allows a knowledge base to broaden and become more accurate. Learning classroom content with the help of feedback and error correction is necessary because these are absolute musts for mastery of complex learning. The brain comes to understand complex information over a period of time. It creates rough drafts, so to speak, during the learning process (Eichenbaum, 2004). These drafts are sketchy, highly inaccurate representations of the material that is held in different areas of the brain until we have a reason to either forget the learning or elaborate on it. In short, we can't store everything, so there's got to be a pretty good reason to move it around and then store it as new learning. For the brain, that good reason usually comes in the form of survival or biologically relevant opportunities. For example, finding a new mate, avoiding conflict, preserving friendships, and getting resources are all examples of important learning. Savvy teachers know that learning must feel personal, compelling, emotional, or urgent if they are going to get students on board.

A Case for Feedback Styles

How does feedback work in the brain? It tells the brain to excite certain cells and to suppress the firing in other cells. What some cells have learned *not* to do is often as important as what other cells have learned *to* do. The process of applying constructive, negative feedback to the learning propels it faster than simply acknowledging a good effort. With positive feedback, students only get a "stroke" when the success or learning has already occurred. No correction is necessary because it does not improve future learning.

Why might negative feedback be better than positive feedback in many cases? The brain weights negative feedback more strongly and remembers it better than positive feedback. In fact, negative information more strongly influences people's future learning than comparable positive information (Peeters & Czapinski, 1990). With negative feedback, you get it before the potential moment of success, so the experience of failure is locked in for future reference to help ensure that you'll avoid it next time. In short, you are getting smarter in one case, but not in another.

The positive reinforcement method is great for boosting morale, but only the process of making mistakes and correcting them will orient learners toward the best solution. Learning by mistake rather than by being given an immediate solution works best in a safe environment. However, as with many principles, you find the right type of feedback in the details.

There are countless ways to organize and label the types of feedback. One of the more common ones is to determine whether the feedback you give is *local* (specific to a small restricted focus) or *global* (generalized to the whole). In addition, there is feedback that is specific to the person ("Here's what you did wrong [or right]") and feedback that is oriented to the task ("The AB function has to end up on the right side of the equation"). As you might guess from this model, *local negative feedback* is most effective and *global negative feedback* is least effective. Positive feedback falls in the middle. Feedback is much less effective when it draws attention to general performance or a global orientation. It is most effective when it draws attention to the task itself, not the person doing it (Kluger & DeNisi, 1996).

Using Feedback Types

Feedback must be the right general type. According to a Columbia University study of fifth graders, praising intelligence actually made students work less, experience less enjoyment, and have less persistence in tasks (Mueller & Dweck, 1998). Praise often makes students feel uncomfortable, especially when it's global and directed at the person ("You're so clever, I *know* you'll do well on this test"). Praising students for effort, on the other hand, had just the opposite effect (Mueller & Dweck, 1998).

Students usually see their intelligence as a fixed item that they have little to do with, and it's often as much of a burden as it is a blessing. However, effort is highly variable, and students appreciate getting noticed when they do make an effort, especially for a tough curriculum. In general, feedback is better when it is specific and corrective. Students get little out of feedback unless it helps them understand how and why their response was not accurate.

Brains rarely get it right the very first time

Expect to correct & accuracy will climb

Using only one type of feedback is limiting. Don't get vested in just one or two specific types of feedback. Lee and Francis (1994) examined the effects of different feedback strategies on achievement and attitude development with 165 college students. Different levels of feedback strategies worked differently for each student, and yet they all ended up with the same final result in improving student achievement. Accept that variety is necessary, and make it a habit to rotate strategies in order to reach more students. For some, it may be as simple as summarizing the material, which works well to deepen the learning (Hattie, Biggs, & Purdie, 1996; Levin, 1988).

Impersonal feedback is less effective than personal feedback. In fact, in one study (Riccomini, 2002), students' performances were significantly better on the criterion task when they received feedback from a live instructor as compared to Web-based feedback. Students like actually hearing the words spoken. In another study (Huang, 2000), all students got the same feedback, but one group got it in written form and the other got

Feedback Strategies I

---

1. Building a model, comparing it to your own work. The model can be a physical one or a visual one drawn, but the model will have to match up with a standard provided.

2. Doing a gallery walk with feedback. Students will post their work, then others will develop a rubric for making constructive comments. Then, they take a walk and post constructive comments.

3. Doing author's chair. Allow the student to sit as the author (with other students surrounding him or her) to answer questions about the work he or she has written.

4. Games with competition (keep score and have fun). These can be simple ones with a *Jeopardy!* format, *Let's Make a Deal,* Trivial Pursuit, or any other format you like.

5. Hypothesis building and trying it out. It can be done in abstract or concrete.

6. Peer editing. Student work gets passed to others who have clear criteria for evaluating it.

7. Student presentations with audience feedback.

---

it in the form of an audio recording. Those who heard the feedback were far happier than those who read it. This does not mean that all feedback needs to come from you personally; it can come from peers, outside experts, or other role models at school or home.

Simplified, less feedback is better at the start. Different tasks have different requirements for feedback. Goodman, Wood, and Hendrickx (2004) found that too much feedback at the start of a task limits students' exploratory tendencies and causes students to rein in their curiosity. It seems that if a task requires a more open-ended approach, early feedback ought to be minimal. Give too much and the brain may overload and performance drops (Schroth, 1997). It is better to offer more later in the refined stages. Instructive feedback (versus the right/wrong type) gives a wider variety of information in response to students' work, which produces measurable improvements in learning (Latham, 1997).

Negative is better, but stress is a significant factor in feedback effectiveness. Learning what we did wrong can be stressful for some, and it is important to recognize this. We all respond differently to feedback, and for the most part, we'd rather get positive than negative feedback. But we don't learn as fast or as accurately with positive feedback only. We need

Feedback Strategies II

---

8. Think, pair, share, and get feedback. This can be done once an hour to keep ideas fresh.

9. Use audio/video recording, discussion, and feedback. The later playback of student behaviors will surprise just about everyone—a great learning experience.

10. Use a graphic organizer. Students assemble the ideas/content from yesterday and get feedback.

11. Using a fishbowl process. When a team or group is ready, allow another team or group to circle, watch, listen, and reflect them and listen in on the discussion to learn from them.

12. Check against an agreed upon standard. It may be one from a text, website, or rubric, but it will give clear guidelines.

13. Homework. Give small defined quantities (10 min. worth).

14. Pretesting (before every unit). This will give students a clear idea of what you are looking for and also provide feedback for them to assess their prior knowledge.

---

negative feedback. Negative information more strongly influences learning than comparably extreme positive information (Peeters & Czapinski, 1990). There's also a much greater change in motivational output from negative feedback. Students who are more resilient and have a healthy ability to regulate stress and strong emotional coping skills will respond better to direct feedback.

Keep the effects of stress in mind as you provide feedback to your students:

- **Timing**: Students who already carry a higher stress load or have anxiety, depression, or trauma issues will be more sensitive to feedback. Give them more "cushioned" feedback, or slightly delayed feedback, and ensure that it is all about the task, not the person.
- **Who**: Many students are more responsive (in a positive way) to teacher comments, and others are more responsive to peer comments. Be sure to provide a variety of sources for feedback.
- **Format**: Interactive is better (not just a few bullets or comments by a teacher). During conversations, use student-generated rubrics and write follow-up notes (Hyland, 1998).
- **Relative standing**: Although there are a few highly competitive students who crave to know their class standings or rankings, for

the most part students find that information very stressful. Therefore, avoid class comparisons; use criteria or individual goals instead. It is far better to ask "Where are you now compared to a month ago?" than it is to make comparisons to the class at large. Standard deviations, Z scores, and class rankings have got to go; evidence shows that they don't motivate students and only the teachers are impressed with the math behind them (Kluger & DeNisi, 1996).

Practical Strategies for Providing Consistent Feedback

First of all, receiving some feedback is better than receiving none. Ensure that some feedback is offered at least every 30 minutes, every single day. Here are the key issues to keep in mind:

- Use regular, weekly, expected quizzes.
- A variety of feedback is optimal.
- Reliable feedback quality is essential.
- Use feedback in timely manner.

Feedback Strategies III

---

15. Rubrics. These can be developed first by the teacher, then slowly students learn what factors need to be a part of it.

16. Weekly scheduled quiz. Make one day per week a designated quiz day. Students and teachers each submit 50% of the questions.

17. Parent or neighbor feedback. Students can bounce ideas and theories off others and refine them for class time.

18. Small group discussion. When the group discussion is led by a trained leader, or the group is given a template for give and take, all can get valuable feedback on their own ideas.

19. Brainstorming. The very act of throwing out ideas which later get analyzed gives you feedback on how well others can process your ideas.

20. Journal writing. The teacher can read and comment on daily blogs, poetry, diary entries, and short stories.

21. Experiments. Use common household items so that kids can learn about cause and effect, critical thinking, and prediction skills.

What Makes Feedback Work So Well?

Working with a group of 56 sixth graders, McCarthy (1995) had students perform verb-recognition tests with pre- and posttests. The results indicated that feedback greatly facilitated improved posttest performance and increased near-transfer performance as well. But feedback does not have to be direct from teacher to student. Embedded feedback works as well as overt feedback. Farragher and Yore (1997) found that high school students improved their learning of science texts when they received feedback imbedded in assignments, monitoring questions from the teacher, and regulating prescriptive feedback.

The packaging of feedback is important. Students can learn well from each other if the feedback session is well structured (Soler, 2003). Students prefer different types of feedback (e.g., peer tutoring, small-group sharing, role-playing, games); some would rather be told—some directly, some indirectly—and others need to see the feedback as a note, a quiz, or a grade. Make absolutely sure you use a variety of feedback styles to cater to various learners' needs. Be sure students can implement the feedback the next time they complete a similar task. Telling a student that she missed 12 questions on a quiz is nearly useless. What does work are small study teams that debrief about the test together, learn from it, and even keep a journal on strategies for next time. Then follow up on this group work with a more authoritative teacher presentation at the end. Participation will go up, and the fact that students got feedback first from their peers will soften the teacher presentation (which may illuminate the mistakes; Bobby et al., 2004).

Prompt feedback is better than later feedback. In a study with 97 fifth graders, each took a multiple-choice test with factual and guess questions after reading a 900-word text (Peeck, van den Bosch, & Kreupeling, 1985). Then students received one of three types of feedback about their performance: immediate and informative, delayed, or none at all. As you might guess, the ones who got the most immediate feedback did better. In studies with college students, the quick nature of the feedback seemed to be instrumental in improving performance with an online task (Phye & Sanders, 1994) or with instructor-delivered feedback (Riccomini, 2002). Just as important, do not wait until quizzes or tests to make sure students get feedback. Use multiple formats to ensure that feedback is continuous.

Starting feedback early in a child's education is good. Willoughby, Porter, Belsito, and Yearsley (1999) found that it's useful at all ages, including early grades. Don't wait too long on the feedback—sooner is better. Give short, succinct task feedback early on. The learning curve is the steepest at the beginning. Over time, as mistakes are made and corrections are made, the errors become smaller and the performance improves. For early learners, focus on one error at a time, and allow the child time for correction. Frequency of feedback usually works best.

Feedback should be reliable. Expected feedback is better than surprises. At Florida State University and Ohio State's Academic Learning Lab, Bruce Tuckman did experiments with college-age students. Students who took announced weekly quizzes were compared to two other groups of students with comparable aptitude: those who were assigned homework on the same material, and a control group that neither took spot quizzes nor completed homework assignments. On the final achievement tests, the quiz group outperformed the homework group by 16 percent and the control group by 24 percent (Tuckman, 1999). Who did better, then? Among the higher-performing students, both homework and spot quizzes helped. Grades rose dramatically for students with lower GPAs when they studied for a quiz every week. Was it the feedback or the stress of the test that improved learning? That's a difficult question, and the answer may be both.

Optimal Feedback

Summary of what we have learned

1. Localized is better than global

2. Task specific is better than personal

3. Simple is better than complex

4. Mix both types (positive and negative)

5. A bit too much is better than too little

6. Best to apply toward the middle of the task

7. Personalized is better than impersonal

8. Have it more often, not less often

9. Mix up strategies to reach more

10. Make the good news public (not the bad)

The process of improving achievement works better with regular (usually weekly) but not unexpected quizzes. Give students a term-long schedule of announced quizzes, and they will perform better (Ruscio, 2001; Thorne, 2000). Teachers should refrain from punishing a class with unannounced pop quizzes because these raise anxiety levels (Nitko, 2001) and are incompatible with the brain's relationship to learning. For teachers and students alike, advance notice and content preparation are the keys to success.

SUMMARY

A final note about feedback: it takes time to debrief, process, and reflect. Avoid rushing this process because it may be the most valuable part of the day for learners who are trying to improve themselves. Learners need time after they've discovered their mistakes in order to conceptualize them, generalize them, make applicable rules, and write them down or share them with another student. Without the debriefing, feedback gets lost in the shuffle. Fierce teaching means having the humility to admit that your teaching won't get into students' heads right the first time and the integrity and commitment to fix it and get it right with error correction.

Strategy 3

Input-to-Output Ratio

WHO'S DOING THE LEARNING?

Simple learning takes no time at all. Put your hand on a hot stove, and you'll learn fast. But for complex explicit learning (e.g., words, text, ideas), the brain needs to take it in, evaluate it, make meaning of it, and even try it out. There must be more student output than teacher or text input. To maximize your students' learning, remember the 51–49 rule: your talking should never exceed 51 percent of class time. This simple ratio contrasts with teachers who often lecture for more than 90 percent of total class time. But remember, this book is about maximizing learning, not maintaining "old school" dogma. The brain needs enough processing time to make and strengthen connections that are the foundation and structure of learning.

The Truth About Time in Learning

More content per minute and faster learning of the content is not better than less content per minute. Both physiologically and emotionally, time is an essential ingredient for mastery of learning. It's clear that no one becomes a master at something instantly. Even child prodigies throughout history were notorious for their endless hours of practice to develop mastery. For example, Beethoven's early interest in and passion for music fueled the work ethic necessary for his early excellence. At school, we're not usually concerned with developing the next icon in musical history, but we at least want good learning.

Research shows correlations between brain development and actual time spent engaged in complex learning (Jacobs, Schall, & Scheibel, 1993). Give students enough time during learning, at the end of learning, and over a period of days, weeks, and months in order to get the learning right. There's no replacement for time; developing any kind of mastery takes time. For new classroom learning, a good motto is "Too much, too fast, it won't last."

Mastery of Material Through Time

Ericsson (1996), who has studied the development of mastery or expertise, says it's going to take time, no matter how you slice it. To become a track star, musician, chess player, or content master, it takes at least 10,000 hours. We don't expect students to get to that level of mastery in school, but we have to acknowledge that with the curriculum that is offered, there is no way any student at school is going to gain mastery of much at all. The curriculum is a mile wide and an inch deep. The time needed for mastery comes in many forms so that students are able to do the following:

- take in the initial new information that eventually becomes background
- regulate or adjust to the rate of incoming learning
- make mistakes and correct them
- make the physical connections in the brain
- develop complex or explicit hierarchies of understanding
- integrate the connections made with related learning
- develop comfort with the knowledge or skill by way of unconscious competence

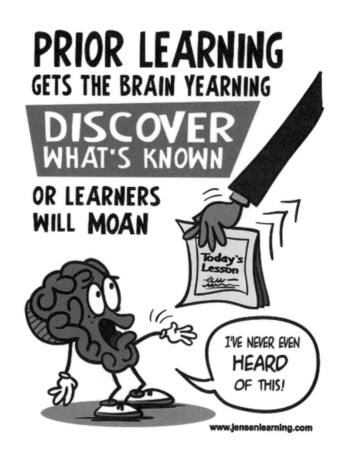

Out of all the variables for developing mastery, the input-to-output ratio may be one of the most frustrating. Pressured by standards, focused by high-stakes testing, and limited by time, many educators seem determined to cram one more fact, skill, or test answer into the school day.

The Brain's Perspective on Learning

Internal factors in the brain regulate the potential speed in learning. Assuming that two students have similar knowledge (which they never do) and the subject material is of equal novelty and complexity, physiology becomes relevant. Here are just four (of many) factors that illuminate the *why* of the 51–49 percent rule:

- limitations in working memory
- consolidating the learning
- hippocampus overload
- cortical limitations

Limitations in Working Memory

Each student has unique limitations on his or her working memory, which has to juggle the new input while making some coherence out of it. The old notion was that we could hold the magical number seven, plus or minus two. New research suggests we are lucky to hold just four chunks (Cowan, 2001). A great deal of other evidence supports the idea that there are significant limitations on what students can hold in their heads (Callicott et al., 1999; Klingberg, 2000; Lachter & Hayhoe, 1995). This mental juggling is known as the *cognitive load theory*. Research suggests that we be cautious with the rate of delivery of instructional information (Carlson, Chandler, & Sweller, 2003).

Consolidating the Learning

Different types of learning require a different amount of time to stabilize. Surprisingly, the amount of time needed to connect, stabilize, and strengthen a memory ranges from several minutes (not seconds) to several hours (Dudai, 2004). Just to record and remember where things are, hippocampal neurons require five to six minutes of experience to form stable spatial representations (Frank, Stanley, & Brown, 2004). Typically, it takes 15 to 60 minutes for the synapse to form and become stable for most explicit learning. The majority of the brain's connection points that are formed at the synapse (the extending presynaptic boutons and subsequent synaptic adhesion) are stable in efficacy and position over a period of 90 minutes (Hopf, Waters, Mehta, & Smith, 2002). Most complex implicit learning—primarily skill learning—requires up to six hours of settling time to solidify (Shadmehr & Holcomb, 1997). Synapses stay intact partly

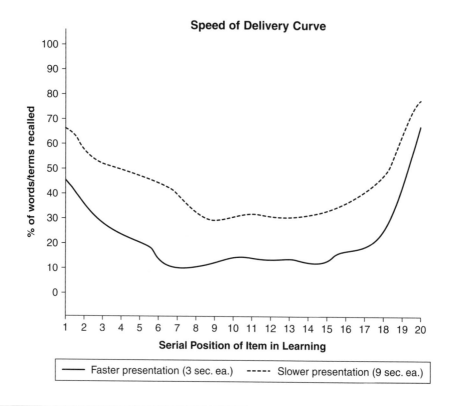

Speed of Delivery Curve

SOURCE: Sumby, 1965.

through synaptic adhesion, a process that binds the connecting axon and dendrite together. At this time, researchers do not know whether different learning in different areas of the brain would constitute "competing" stimuli. But it is clear that too much information constitutes an overload similar to attempts to write new information to a CD after it's already full.

Hippocampus Overload

It seems that the hippocampus tends toward conserving existing information and prevents new learning from resulting in content overload. If the learning is not emotional or relevant and not heard from again, the hippocampus might not even encode it. Repetition of content, even in just an hour, greatly increases its chances of being remembered (Colicos & Goda, 2001). New information may travel the route of working memory to the hippocampus and await further information regarding saliency. The hippocampus becomes the temporary holding and organizing area for all new explicit learning. Sometimes the hippocampus holds information for hours, sometimes for weeks, before letting it go or distributing it to the rest of the cortex for long-term memory (Wiltgen, Brown, Talton, & Silva, 2004).

The hippocampus does not have unlimited storage space. It learns fast, but it is more like a wobbly flash memory stick than a huge hard drive. In a nutshell, here are the facts about the hippocampus:

- It acts as both a surge protector and a trainer to the cortex.
- It's a fast learner with a small capacity.
- It holds and evaluates new explicit information for hours, some-times days.
- It develops representations of the input and back-projects it to the cortex for storage.
- Too much learning overloads networks, and the new information overwrites the old.

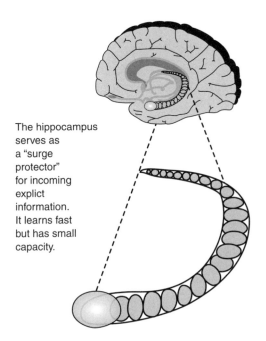

The hippocampus serves as a "surge protector" for incoming explict information. It learns fast but has small capacity.

Cortical Limitations

The fourth and last factor related to the 51–49 rule may surprise you. The growing human brain juggles many new processes as it develops, and there is a massive amount of simultaneous new skill development in the emo-tional, social, physical, and cognitive areas of the brain. Children don't know what's really important to learn except what adults say is important and worth learning. There remains the possibility that very ambitious early school cramming with endless content may lead to some neural crowding effects. This can lessen the flexibility for new learning later on. It might be no coincidence that Albert Einstein was quite average as a school student in his early years. Too much "dumping of curriculum" on children may lead to an early decrease in the size and number of brain regions that are unspeci-fied, but may be necessary for later creativity in the adolescent and adult.

Peter Huttenlocher was a professor of pediatrics and neurology at the University of Chicago before retiring. He had dedicated his life to studying

**What Limits Input
to Students' Brains?**
part 1 of 2

1. **Glucose Available**
   (learning uses it quickly)
2. **Protein Recycling**
   (time *off* task needed)
3. **Working Memory**
   (1–4 chunks or points max.)
4. **Attentional Limits**
   (use student age in minutes)
5. **Synaptic Adhesion**
   (needs 15–60 min.)

synaptic and brain development. Few people understand the growing brain more than he does. He says the neurobiological studies of early brain crowding introduce the caveat that too much early learning may, under some conditions, become detrimental to the learning of later acquired skills. In other words, the wrong real estate gets used up. He adds that

> the brain of the young child may need some "time out" to consolidate the information. Reservation of cortical space for the processing of later acquired skills may also impart a functional advantage. . . . A proper balance of early exposure to an academic enrichment environment and time off may be important for optimal cortical development. (Huttenlocher, 2002)

While this caution may seem a bit crazy, there are many examples of late bloomers in science, music, writing, arts, medicine, and politics. In addition, there are many examples of a child who blooms fast, and his or her parents become convinced that the child is gifted. Then, in the next few years, their child moves to the middle of the academic pack. What if the child's brain was being crowded early and lost the creative room for some later learning? We have to consider that possibility.

**What Limits Input
to Students' Brains?**
part 2 of 2

6. **Hippocampus**
   (overload = "overwrites")
7. **Background Knowledge**
   (tie into prior connections?)
8. **Complexity of Content**
   (schemas in place?)
9. **Novelty of Content**
   (arousing, boring?)
10. **Learning Preference**
    (visual, auditory or tactile)

How Does the Need for Time Translate Into the School Day?

Slavin's (1994) research suggests that achievement gains occur when the classroom improves multiple elements, and time is a critical factor. Marzano is another who has investigated the issue of time available to teach the curriculum required. His team estimated that we need over 15,000 hours (based on the current standards), but we only have about 9,000 hours available, creating a time gap of over 6,000 hours, or six and half years (Marzano, Kendall, & Gaddy, 1999). Clearly, there's too much mandated content. What are our options? We could ask students to spend more time on some subjects and leave out others. For example, in one study, when students got to spend more time on mathematics, they did better (Aksoya & Link, 2000). But realistically, other subjects would get short-changed.

Could teachers leave out extraneous information and increase the density of the content? So far, this has not been shown to work. Increasing the number of facts, the new information per hour, only decreases retention (Russell, Hendricson, & Herbert, 1984). What about slowing down the pace at school to allow more time for reflection? This suggestion has been made and has some merit (C. Wood, 2002). In fact, when college professors pause every few minutes to let students collect their thoughts, subsequent exam scores improve as much as a letter grade (Ruhl, Hughes, & Schloss, 1987). But we still haven't solved the problem—too much content and too little time in which to teach it.

The Importance of Rest Time

Research shows that rest and sleep are invaluable to the learning process. Many researchers have found strong correlations between the amount of sleep and the retained learning (Stickgold, Fosse, & Walker, 2002). Simple learning seems unaffected by mild to moderate REM sleep loss. But complex learning, especially when it involves rules of logic, becomes impaired significantly by sleep loss. Creativity is enhanced by getting enough sleep (Stickgold & Walker, 2004).

Adolescents are especially vulnerable to sleep loss because of other age-related vulnerabilities, such as anxiety disorders, peer pressure, academics, sports, and wide hormone fluctuations (Wolfson & Carskadon, 2003). Students with attention deficit hyperactivity disorder typically get less sleep than their peers and may have difficulty encoding new learning. This suggests the importance of frequent review and consolidation.

Unless students get enough sleep (six to nine hours), their brains may not be able to sufficiently encode the previous day's learning. Compromised sleep has an especially negative effect on adolescents' learning (Dahl, 1999). Remind students about the role of sleep in learning, suggesting that getting enough of it may help them learn more efficiently.

Practical Suggestions to Minimize Information Overload

Although many instructional strategies can reduce the effects of information overload, the brain still has its limits. The brain is better at processing coherent, relevant new information in small bytes for processing and storage. While we can only make suggestions to students about the value of sleep, there are things over which we have more influence. Here is what we can do:

1. Start with a reasonable, doable curriculum in the time allotted. Without it, everything else is a temporary measure until policymakers come to their senses.

2. Use short chunks of learning. Produce new content every 10 minutes, then allow 10 to 15 minutes of processing time. Repeat the cycle. Space out the learning over time.

3. Double back if you really want to keep talking; at least it won't be new information. Use a more spiraling, previewing, and reviewing strategy (Bower, 1987).

4. When presenting new material, simply pause more often. Once every 30 to 60 seconds will allow students' brains time to better assimilate new information (Di Vesta & Smith, 1979). Allow more wait time and more think time for processing (Stahl, 1994).

5. Daytime naps are good (Mednick et al., 2002; Mednick, Nakayama, & Stickgold, 2003). If that's impossible then a brief closed-eye break can work miracles (Maquet, Peigneux, Laureys, & Smith, 2002).

6. Prepare learners better with both content and process priming. This allows them to better assimilate new information.

7. Use continual reviews to strengthen existing learning.

8. Provide mini breaks for stretching, reflection, or movement. Use an energizer to raise blood flow and give students' brains a break.

9. Give half-filled-in notes that provide key words to remember.

10. Use enough variety in your teaching so that students rarely recognize that they're constantly transforming the learning into different understandings.

SUMMARY

Teachers often get in the habit of talking. Step back from this role, and allow students to become the automatic prompts for time or activities to break up the pacing. And remember that speeding up the teaching means more content is covered but is not necessarily memorable. The faster the teaching, the faster the forgetting. The fierce teacher is one who respects the limitations of the brain and allows sufficient rest time.

Strategy 4

Elaboration for Depth

Over time, countless instructional models have been introduced to educators. One model seems particularly popular: quickly introduce the material once, and then move on. Teachers can make many assumptions about why that happens (e.g., lack of time, testing pressure, ignorance), but the bottom line is that students will never get to the mastery level unless they elaborate on and explore their material and then develop coherence and meaning. In a way, elaboration creates depth, and feedback corrects the elaboration. The fierce teacher insists on making time for elaboration and avoids the throw-out-content-and-run strategy so commonly found in schools today.

The old paradigm was that if learners pay attention, they should get it right. A more accurate paradigm is "Assume that your students are not getting it, and then work from that as a baseline." To get to mastery, students need opportunities and guidance to deepen their learning and explore the topic in depth. The fierce teacher makes this a key part of the overall lesson plan.

WHAT IS ELABORATION?

Not all learning is worth elaboration. Elaboration is not practice, nor is it repetitive. Instead of being horizontal, it's vertical. It's the digging to flesh out the content and get it right. The process of elaboration is the means by which students (a) do the thinking needed for the big picture, (b) dig for details, (c) look for connections, and (d) find meaning in the learning.

In the brain, the difference between simple learning and elaborative learning is easy to show. Simple learning means fewer connections and less dendritic branching. Complex learning means more dendrites that are longer and have more spines for connecting. The brain is different when students have elaborated on content, but it is the process of elaboration—the satisfaction of actually learning something well—that's as valuable as being able to write or talk about the content later.

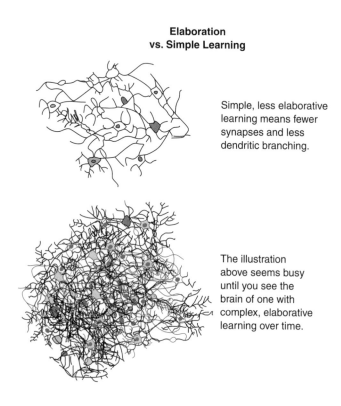

**Elaboration
vs. Simple Learning**

Simple, less elaborative learning means fewer synapses and less dendritic branching.

The illustration above seems busy until you see the brain of one with complex, elaborative learning over time.

Preparation for Elaborative Learning

Let's explore ways to make it happen in your classroom. First, make a promise to yourself that when at all possible and whenever appropriate, you'll offer elaborative time to students. Second, access to content is critical. Students who have to ask permission to use materials, wait for others to lend it out, or lack Internet access will likely have less background knowledge and have difficulty with elaborative strategies (Willoughby et al., 1999). Prepare for bringing more to the table yourself. Titsworth's (2001) study used scripted, videotaped lectures to test the effects of teacher immediacy (high vs. low), use of organizational cues (with cues vs. without cues), and student note taking (took notes vs. did not take notes). All of the cues, prompts, and notes helped, and the students gained greater in-depth mastery.

Elaboration Categories

There are hundreds of potential strategies, but here are examples of the larger processing categories for students:

- Processing for width: Broaden their learning with more surface, but much broader understanding.
- Processing for depth: Deepen learning by finding more details and more complete understandings.
- Processing for perspective: Go after the material by taking on a new point of view to gain more diversity of understanding.
- Processing to make meaning: Find ways that the material connects to them personally.
- Processing to package and communicate: Turn the content into a video or other multimedia presentation.
- Processing for application: Find and demonstrate specific practical applications for the material.
- Processing through individual, personal reflection: Provide structures for doing this, and allow time during the lesson as well as afterward for sharing.

The "How-to" of Elaboration

Getting students to become more skillful at (and sold on) processing takes time. You'll need to demonstrate it, model it, and provide frameworks for it. These are the commonly used processing steps:

- Vesting: Get the student to care about the task. (See the discussion of vesting in Chapter 1.)
- Modeling solutions: Show that there are solutions and even better ones than first thought. Students will be more likely to continue if they can already do the task one way.
- Simplifying: Break the task into mini tasks that are easily understood and accomplishable.
- Maintaining student engagement: Keep students focused on the goal through encouragement.
- Ensuring feedback: Although your feedback doesn't have to be the sole source, it offers a contrast between current and desired progress.
- Managing states: Students can get frustrated. Support the process by which they learn to ask for help or simply to work through it.

Five Elaboration Strategies

The potential elaboration strategies listed here are just a few of the hundreds possible. Let's explore five easy-to-use strategies:

- in-depth discussions and summaries
- reciprocal teaching
- student-generated assessments
- elaborative question-and-answer time
- elaborative visual thinking

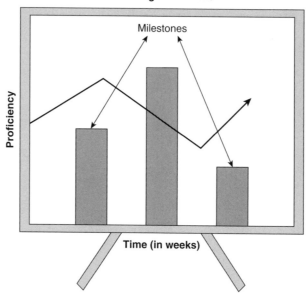

**Complex Content or Skill
Learning Takes Time**

Learning does not progress on a continual upward slope. Skills are built up, sustained for a while, then they often collapse and are rebuilt all over again. *Deeper learning takes time.*

SOURCE: Fischer, 2000.

In-depth discussions and summaries. There is no replacement for this strategy. Students need to talk about, argue, think through, summarize, question, rewrite, and recall the learning to develop some depth of elaboration. Eysenck and Eysenck (1979) showed that processing capacity is greater when information is retrieved from secondary memory (the resource) than when it is retrieved from primary memory ("I recall . . ."). Allow students to uncover details within the main ideas from content searches; many key ideas may have a half-dozen subtopics, and each of those may have another dozen details. Keep adding what's learned to the notes until the level of detail is just right. Remember, students have to do the digging, not you. The person in your classroom who is working the hardest at learning is doing the most learning. This does not mean that teachers don't need to work; it simply reminds you that it's a good day for students when they leave class pretty worn out from digging, exploring, asking, sorting, and writing.

Reciprocal teaching. Research supports reciprocal teaching. Developed by Annemarie Palincsar and Ann Brown (1984), reciprocal teaching switches the roles of the student and teacher. These are the three basic steps (Coleman, Rivkin, & Brown, 1997):

- **Group discussions:** Smaller groups allow less competent students to perform at higher levels with greater safety than in the large group.

- **Independent group discussions:** The group collaborates to revise, understand, and construct the meaning of the material in its own way. Students become motivated by autonomy and curiosity.
- **Scaffolding:** Students can learn from peers just as well as they can from adults. But the process must be guided and managed to avoid any downsides. Provide support for less competent students, and then back off.

Student-generated assessments. Students get more in depth by having to formulate quality questions about the material. Let students create quizzes, summaries, or dialogues with the material. Recently, teachers have found that if you pause and give students time to answer questions on index cards, and then discuss in groups, learning increases. These short in-class writing exercises increase focus, thinking, and depth of knowledge (Butler, Phillmann, & Smart, 2001).

Elaborative question-and-answer time. The old way was to ask students for their answers, acknowledge them, and move on. But research tells us that asking students to explain *why* the answer is correct is better. For students to grow as thinkers and gatherers of knowledge and to improve self-esteem, make the typical question-and-answer process more productive. Ask students to explain why correct answers are right and why and how they came up with the incorrect answers. Doing so consistently leads to deeper, more accurate learning (Bielaczyc, Pirolli, & Brown, 1995). If you compare the results of high school student learning with complete materials provided versus self-generated elaborations, students demonstrate greater learning when instructed to use self-generated and very elaborative interrogation (a questioning strategy using *why* questions). The other, less effective choice is to use repetition of teacher-provided elaborations of facts (Wood, 1994).

Teachers must keep a class going, in spite of plenty of distractions. Keeping students engaged in fast questioning means students can give answers in a short amount of time; the teacher feels that class is "moving along," but it's not. Most pupils won't even try to think carefully about their response. They know that either there's no time for a deeper one or someone else will chime in if they don't. After all, just a few pupils in a class answer the teacher's questions; the rest stay out of that risky fray, knowing that they cannot respond as quickly and being unwilling to risk making mistakes in public. If the teacher keeps the question-and-answer session snappy and quick by lowering the level of questions and by accepting answers from a few students, then everyone loses. Better ideas include the following:

- Ask students for their answer with a lower time limit—they must talk about it for at least 30 seconds at the elementary level and 60 seconds at the secondary level.

- Ask questions, then allow students time to talk over the answer with a buddy and, when you call on them, to both stand and discuss their answer.
- Give questions the day before, and make them the homework assignment. Have students prepare a 60-second response that can be used in class; they must be able to defend it, too.
- Listen for all responses, and don't indicate whether they are right or wrong; simply thank students for their responses and have someone record them on the board. Record 10 to 15 possible responses, then put students in groups and let them vote on which answers are better and why.
- Always use the question-and-answer time for elaboration. Take every opportunity you can to elaborate, even in front of the room.
- Remember that students are highly sensitive to your comments, so be on your best behavior when asking students to elaborate.

Elaborative visual thinking. Many have advocated the use of visual thinking as a tool for elaboration. This may include murals, posters, drawings, computer graphics, paintings, and mapping. As a generalization, this type of thinking lends itself well to elaboration because words and pictures can be highly detailed. It forces content organizing, fact checking, and even checking for relationships spatially. In addition, students can learn to do transformation of content (e.g., turn a summary into a song, turn an object into a mural, map it). Visual thinking is a great learning tool.

Brigham and Scruggs (1995) measured college students' memory based on their recollection of familiar and unfamiliar animals using visual or verbal elaboration strategies. Students who used imagery organized unfamiliar animal information much better than those who used verbal elaboration. Your students may also discover a new organization of content (see it in a larger context, see categories within it), or they may see the content the same, but discover new meaning from the same content (study, discussion, or reflection may bring it out). Using visual strategies, students often gain a new understanding of the critical and most key relationships (e.g., water-clouds-rain) in the content.

The fact is that there are countless ways that students can go deeper into the learning. But without having some guidelines about where elaboration can take students cognitively, you won't know what kind of elaboration to use. The five categories just discussed are a good starting point. Focus on just one at a time overtly, but use others more covertly. For example, add a reflection activity once a week, then put students in small groups and let them share selected entries with each other (Williams & Wessel, 2004). This processing time will reduce the sense of being overwhelmed by content for those students who have low background knowledge, missed a class, or have not done homework. Over time, students will begin to be more receptive of feedback. The key is to provide a variety of deliberate, guided practice (Moulaert, Verwijnen, Rikers, & Scherpbier, 2004).

Elaboration is not an instant or two-minute sponge activity. Essential aspects of deliberate practice are the presence of well-defined tasks, informative feedback, repetition, self-reflection, motivation, and endurance. Studies have shown a positive relation between deliberate practice and level of expertise. In this case, the time spent is as important as the appropriateness of a single activity.

Elaboration Alternatives

So far we've discussed auditory elaboration and visual elaboration. These are your primary tools because you can get into far greater detail and explain the detail with those two modalities. But remember, many of your students are going to want to elaborate on the material in other domains of skill. You may want to provide your class with the option of kinesthetic elaboration after the other ones have been implemented. This approach includes the use of role-plays, simulations, building models, hands-on demonstrations, drama, or even dance. Many teachers see these activities as far from hardcore academics, remember that I suggest implementing these only after students have already done the elaboration and are ready to produce a product for grading.

Practical Suggestions for Follow-Up

Fortunately, there's no limit to the number of activities that promote deeper, more accurate learning. Yet the follow-up after the elaboration with feedback is the key. For example, you can use checklists or encourage peer feedback to improve learning in English as a second language classrooms (Furneaux, 2002). Students' learning improves when their memory uses processes, constructions, or generations (Levin, 1988). (Find more examples of error-correction in Strategy 2 on pages 17–19.)

Elaboration with built-in feedback is key to the process. Here are some examples:

- building a hypothesis, trying it out, and then debriefing it
- building a model, and then comparing it to another
- peer editing
- think-pair-share activities, followed by feedback
- using audio recording, discussing, and then getting feedback
- building a model, and trying its functionality
- doing a gallery walk with feedback
- giving student presentations, with audience feedback
- playing games with competition
- using a video or mirror to watch, reflect, and discuss
- doing author's chair or fishbowl processes
- using a checklist to measure results

SUMMARY

Highly effective teachers have figured out elaborative processes and use them often. Make the assumption that once you've got learners vested and engaged, they still won't get it right the first time. They won't be at the level of depth necessary to either be excited about the content or be able to pass an exam on it. They'll need plenty of opportunities to elaborate and get feedback. This chapter has offered both details and guidelines for providing constructive feedback without triggering too much stress. But the simple concept of elaborating on the learning is a staple in the fierce teacher's strategic toolbox.

Strategy 5

Recall and Memory Management

The primary evidence of classroom learning is memory. If students are exposed to learning, but don't encode or recall it, the job's not finished. Recall and purposeful memory encoding is simply good for learning. It strengthens connections in the brain. Recall and purposeful memory encoding is a must-have condition for mastery or complex learning because without it learners lack the basis for growth. It creates solidarity and a sense of "knowingness" in learning. We build new and more complex learning on the strength of simple known structures with which we are already comfortable. If your students learn it and forget it, did they really learn it? The fierce teacher is one who does not just teach; he or she teaches to get it remembered.

WHAT MAKES PURPOSEFUL MEMORY ENCODING SO GOOD?

The old school of thought believed that exposure to an idea once meant it was stored. Some thought that storage (or memory) was a bit like a photograph or an audio recording. We now know those analogies were both wrong and misleading. Researchers have discovered that your brain's synapses are not static: they constantly adapt in response to activity (Atwood & Karunannithi, 2002). The reactivation of memories can disrupt and alter memories; hence, memory is not fixed (Nadel & Land, 2000). But the more we use an idea accurately, the more we activate a skill or complete the same process and the smoother, faster, and more accurate we get at it. Once we have repeated a task, our brains become more economical. We use less glucose to do the same task, so it becomes more energy efficient (Haier et al., 1992).

Our working memory temporarily holds brand-new explicit information (e.g., text, story, pictures). Once we decide to use it, it eventually makes its way to the hippocampus, which serves as a staff developer to the brain by training, organizing, then connecting with the appropriate areas of the cortex in the new learning it has saved. Repetition tells the brain, "This is worth saving—keep it!" In fact, recent research suggests that it takes three to four times for the brain to remember most things (Colicos & Goda, 2001). That guideline assumes that no other negative factors are present (e.g., compelling circumstances, intense emotions). The repetition turns the brain from a tangled jungle of neurons into sizzling intellect. Or at least one with a decent memory. When neural connections are stimulated repeatedly, and we pay attention, they strengthen significantly (Kilgard & Merzenich, 1998).

Six Approaches for Repetition to Get Memories Encoded

There are many ways to ensure that learning is encoded, including strong meaning making, engaging intense emotions, embedding physical activity, and repetition. Here the focus is on repetition, and for good reason. It's easy to use and simple to learn strategies for using it. Repetition consists of intentional, multiple exposures to the content or process of prior learning. Note that the word *exposure* is purposely vague. Ideally, it's done in ways that can enhance understanding.

Too much of the same thing can be boring to the learner, though. Many learners prefer novelty to the mundane. The solution? Use the principle of repetition, but under the guise of different approaches, as follows: preexposure, priming, prior knowledge activation, postviewing, guided practice, and revision with links.

Preexposure

Previewing, or preexposure, is purposeful scaffolding, building background knowledge, and beginning the early foundations for learning. The term *preexposure* is becoming more common in the scientific literature, meaning deeper priming, not for minutes or hours, but weeks, months, or even years in advance. When a second-grade teacher is teaching the times tables, he or she is preexposing learners to something that they'll need much later on in both schooling and real life. This strategy can have effects for months and years in advance (Cave, 1997).

Preexposure is a way to enable the brain's network to avoid having to replace structures acquired earlier during familiarization with brand-new, more unstable, and possibly inaccurate structures experienced at the formal learning time (Altmann, 2003).

Priming

Priming is exposure to a target item (in any of the senses) in a way that is correlated with a later effect. This persisting effect is known as *repetition priming* because the greater the number of repetitions, the greater the later retrieval (Ochsner, Chiu, & Schacter, 1998).

Brain-imaging scans show that advance knowledge of a forthcoming task activates the dorsolateral prefrontal cortex (DLPFC)—an important problem-solving area located on the outer surface of the frontal lobes (Carter, MacDonald, & Ursu, 2000). Conversely, when the brain does not anticipate having to perform a specific task, the DLPFC remains dormant. It seems to look forward to what it needs to do next in order to perform the task better; the more this area is activated, the better the recall of detailed task procedures. The effects in the brain are real—one can see changes in both electrical and chemical activity (Gratton et al., 1992).

Priming gives improved efficiency to a learner's ability to name a word, an object, or a concept or even to perform a skill based on some earlier exposure (Martin & van Turennout, 2002), and it can have long-term effects (Cave, 1997). For example, you can use semantic priming by saying, "Later this afternoon, we'll be learning how the times tables saved a person's life—stay tuned for that." This expectancy of useful information increases the likelihood of recall (Gratton, Coles, & Donchin, 2002). If you know the key ideas that your learners need to know a week or a month from now, create a summary and put the ideas on a wall poster. After all, why hide critical information from your students? Here are some simple strategies:

- Encourage a student-led overview, students pairing up to introduce contents or coming attractions, student-generated questions, or announcements of upcoming lessons.
- Use vocabulary words, stop, ask the students to repeat them, and then move forward without an explanation except that now they know something new.
- Encourage students to work with advance organizers, ask questions, or generate hypotheses in advance.
- Give just enough of a preview for students to be curious.

Advance organizers can include a complex description, a web, a story, a picture, a map, or a fishbone diagram. Research on the value of advance organizers is mixed (see Kirkland, 1995; Schwartz, Rosenthal, & Wehr, 1998), but action research in the classroom is a good way to know what's right for your students.

Prior Knowledge Activation

The evidence is far more robust on the value of activating prior knowledge than it is on the use of many other aids for repetition, such as advance organizers (Altmann, 2003). When used correctly, this strategy can allow learners to quickly connect what they know to new content, facilitating learning (Kaplan & Murphy, 2000). There are many positives to the engagement of prior knowledge:

- It reinforces what's been learned.
- It validates specific learning, enhancing self-concept.
- It provides opportunities for connections.

Some research findings on activating prior knowledge include the following:

- A strong meta-analysis found that the more students already know, the better they do in school (Dochy, Segers, & Buehl, 1999).
- Activating prior knowledge helps middle school students engage better with "heavy" informational texts (Spires & Donley, 1998).
- This strategy works well with gifted, regular education, and especially special needs learners (Carr & Thompson, 1996).
- Before the unit begins, during the main part of it, and afterwards, even into the next unit, providing bits and pieces of the content (instead of one giant overload in the middle) offers valuable and unique support (Christen & Murphy, 1991).
- With elementary school children, prior knowledge is especially powerful in knowledge-based areas as opposed to skill-based ones (Hayes, Foster, & Gadd, 2003).
- Prior knowledge activation is successful with college students, suggesting that it is a major determiner of new learning (Hambrick, 2003).
- Even with unrelated, more incidental learning, the activation of prior knowledge is valuable (Wattenmaker, 1999).
- A caution: prior knowledge activation can decrease new learning when students believe that they already know what's coming up (S. L. Wood & Lynch, 2002).

Postviewing

This is the process of immediate review after new learning. Postviewing is often embedded in guided practice or in immediate elaboration of the same material. A good comprehension strategy is to ask students to change representations of the new learning. If students just saw a video, they may write about or discuss it. If they just read a passage, use this time for reprocessing with a paired sharing or mapping the material. By jumping in immediately in the moments following content, you can accomplish the following:

- clarify or strengthen learning
- allow for error correction
- establish learners' confidence about the material and themselves

Guided Practice

Guided practice can be exciting. When it's done well, students will look forward to the comfort and stability they can get from daily repetition. At the Children's School at Carnegie Mellon University, the cognitive psychology department designs and runs the instruction. According to Director Sharon Carver (2001), "The consistent repetition of the Children's School daily and weekly routines, as well as the consistent expectations for behavior, increase the strength of their memory and ease of retrievability, which, in turn, sets the stage for children's comfort with and independence in our learning environment."

Practice is best right after a lesson, when the synapses are still forming. Peter Huttenlocher is professor of pediatrics and neurology at the University of Chicago. His work is considered classic in modern neuroscience, particularly his detailed studies on synaptic formation and brain development:

> Parents and children often object to the many repetitions that appear to be built into most school programs. However, the importance of frequent recapitulation and continued practice receives support from knowledge of developmental neurobiology. The abandonment of practicing would be apt to increase the loss of previously acquired information, especially during late childhood and early adolescence. . . . Such review should not be rote repetition. We know from computer simulation of learning in a neural net that the most effective input is varied, but has internal consistency. (Huttenlocher, 2002, p. 212)

Here are some suggestions for guided practice:

- Avoid sending students home to practice and reinforce something they don't know.
- Take the time to practice and correct errors in class.
- Vary your reviews—from student-generated quizzes, to role-plays, to direct application of the content.

With guided practice, students can see the immediate relevance, and they stay interested. As soon as they leave your class, they are already forming a new memory. Make sure it's a true one.

Revision With Links

Over time, nearly all complex learning becomes a revision versus a copy of the original learning. The likelihood of word-for-word or exact concept recall is either rare or simply not going to happen. Our recall for complex learning is much less dependable than earlier thought. Here are some research findings on revision:

Encode for Retrieval

Pre-exposure
Priming
Prior Knowledge
Previews
Review
Revisions
Quizzes

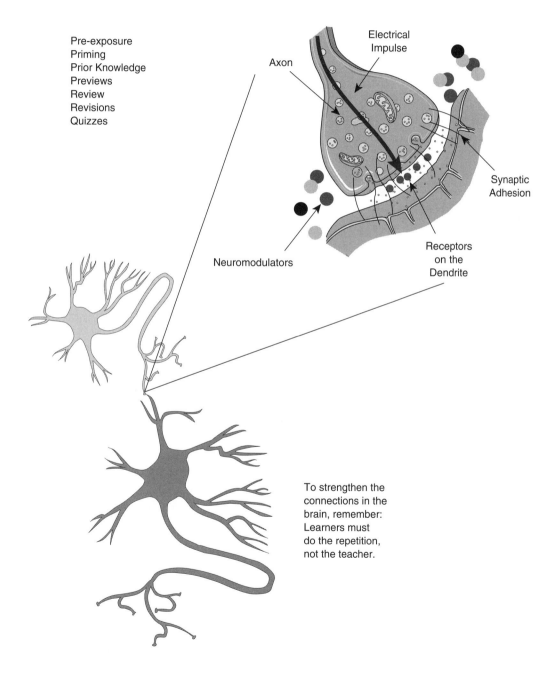

Electrical
Impulse

Axon

Synaptic
Adhesion

Neuromodulators

Receptors
on the
Dendrite

To strengthen the
connections in the
brain, remember:
Learners must
do the repetition,
not the teacher.

- The revision process is the task of reconstructing the learning from hours, days, or weeks ago. It's critical to student performance (Collie, Maruff, Darby, & McStephen, 2003).
- A host of factors lead to significant losses, confusion, distortion, or simple erosion in memory (Schacter, 2001). It makes more sense to call it an update, a renewed version, or a revision. Why? Recall has the ability to corrupt memory.
- Allow students time to continually revise and refresh their learning. Students need to develop a large graphic overview of the material (Wallace, Wandell, West, & Ware, 1998).

Complete "linking" by mapping the previous day's learning. Students can look up material that they're unfamiliar with, and then share their findings with others in pairs or small groups. If it's important, invest in the time for linking. If it's not, skip it.

Practical Suggestions for Effective Repetition and Practice

- To prevent monotony, shift around the types of activities you use. Provide learning brains with advance warning of task changes.
- When soliciting answers to a difficult question, allow sufficient time for learners to formulate a response before calling on anyone.
- Create a learning environment in which students feel comfortable, safe, and smart. Reassure students that making mistakes is how we learn.
- Give students time to do peer editing, browse through their own written material, compare notes with posters on the wall, contrast their work with a neighbor's, or simply think about their learning.
- Students must learn to memorize, without fail, certain things such as the alphabet; times tables; and their name, address, and phone number. Use small groups or fun activities with mnemonics.
- Use priming to introduce vocabulary words. Introduce them formally (a new word every day), and highlight them in discussions.
- Videos, field trips, art, wall posters, music, and special events can prime learning.
- Do fill-in-the-blank activities with your students. For example, "We've been learning about a tool for increasing learning that starts with a *P-r*, and it's called _____ (priming)."
- Organize small groups of three to four students to create questions, fill-in sentences, quizzes, and test questions.
- Do simple choral responses.
- Ask students to create a graphic organizer independently, in small groups, or with partners. Pass each one around the room, and invite others to add to it.
- Ask small groups of students to summarize a key point in a rhyming one-line review. Have them add a little choreography and present it to the class.

SUMMARY

Never assume that students actually know the material unless they can demonstrate it. In fact, assume that they don't know it until they can show, tell, build, teach, or test well on the class work. Try some of the suggestions discussed in this chapter to ensure stronger brain connections. There's a big difference between being familiar with complex learning and truly knowing it. Avoid student boredom or refusals by creating a bit more novelty in the process. Do your own practicing of these activities. The fierce teacher blends prior learning with current learning and primes students for upcoming learning. This process allows students to gain mastery quicker with less effort. Your students will become much more enthusiastic, and their confidence will soar.

Strategy 6

Content Coherence

The world floods us with a constant sensory buffet, and unless we can make some sense of it, we are overwhelmed, baffled, and often frustrated. Watch or listen to someone with severe autism, and you can get a sense of how his or her brain has difficulty making coherence out of the flood of sensory input. Incoming data is overwhelming, often with little or no filtering. It comes across as unorganized, coded, linked, or relevant. This makes it useless and even annoying. As a result, many students become frustrated, angry, or simply shut down and fail the class. The fierce teacher understands the necessity for content coherence, takes responsibility for it, and constantly orchestrates it.

"I couldn't understand my math teacher." "My English teacher may as well be speaking Greek!" Those are typical comments by students who are not "getting it" at school. We've all had teachers who had content mastery, but were unable to make it coherent to us. Teachers must mediate coherence in the learning and empower learners to do the same for themselves. This principle says that one must create coherence in the learning or there will be impaired learning, incorrect learning, or even chaos. It is not just a good idea; it is mandatory for learning. We must be able to make some sense out of incoming data, or we will underperform or quit. Here's a way to recall this concept (pardon the "butchering" of English):

WHAT IS COHERENCE?

The stem word is *cohere,* to stick together. Coherence is a quality wherein the whole is logically or aesthetically consistent with all separate parts. It is also clean, not sloppy; it is harmonious, not discordant; it is credible, not discounted. If the new information is scrambled, incomplete, too complex, poorly illustrated, or lacks flow, students will struggle. Coherence is absolutely essential to all complex learning. It is what brings a sense of

order, balance, unity, and even beauty to the learning. When the learning is coherent, we do more than just read the words; they become alive and meaningful to us. Consider the following paragraph:

> You know when to do it because it's something you do often, and if you don't, things can get backed up. Start with one big collection and pick them up, usually one by one. You decide whether it goes into either one location for immediate action or a different spot to attend to later. If it's the latter one, you can come back to it in about an hour. The immediate one gets your attention for a moment. Normally, you can begin the process and then forget about it for a while. Later, you can get back to it for a moment, then put it into a new place, and forget about it again. Once you're done with this part of the process, you arrange and reclassify according to your memorized system. After these actions are done, give the process some time. Soon, you'll know it's time for you to repeat it.

I'll make two guesses. First, I'll guess that you understood every word in that paragraph. Second, I'll guess that the paragraph was incoherent to you. So . . . comprehension does not equal coherence. By the way, the paragraph was a description of doing laundry, and if I had told you that up front, it would surely have been more understandable, even coherent (though not very riveting).

In the "laundry" paragraph, it wasn't the complexity of the words that mattered, but rather the lack of context. You would have understood the passage if you had known in advance what the topic was. That's what your students need. They need a way to make some kind of meaning. If students can't understand the content, they're likely to think, "I'm stupid" or "This class is stupid."

Coherence and meaning are different. Coherence means simply making sense of the content, whereas meaning entails imbuing the content with value, emotion, or relevance. Something can be coherent, yet meaningless. Show a six-year-old student a picture of a triangle, and it may be coherent, yet meaningless. Allow a six-year-old to use a stick to play the shiny musical triangle, and it may become more meaningful. Students' brains often automatically assign meaning to something far different from what a teacher intended, but coherence is not so automatic. Many teachers have a strong, detailed background in their subject area, yet they are unable to translate that into something simple that students can grasp.

Our need for a coherent world begins early. Environmental coherence matters to us right away. Als et al. (2004) found that they could improve brain function in babies born prematurely, compared to those who went full term (both measured again at nine months), by providing a more coherent environment early on. The early quality of experience before what would have been full term may influence brain development significantly in babies born prematurely. There are structures in the brain that respond to clear order. Kilgard and Merzenich (2002), for example, found an order-sensitivity in the primary auditory cortex, which reinforces the principle that we are naturally more responsive with more coherent input.

Texts With Coherence

We've all had the experience of reading both poorly written texts and well-written ones. Students' coherence increases when they read texts that are concrete and clear (Sadoski, Goetz, & Joyce, 1993). Different types of readers get different results from texts. If a text has low coherence, only learners with high background knowledge will benefit from using it (McNamara & Kintsch, 1996). In fact, they do better on poorly written texts—presumably they work harder at it if their interest is high. Learners with low background knowledge, on the other hand, must have highly coherent texts, or they'll do poorly (McNamara, 2001). This suggests that, right from the first day of class, students are already at different levels and compensatory strategies are needed.

Take, for example, one study involving 160 secondary students (Boscolo & Mason, 2000). The students were divided equally into four groups: (1) high interest, high prior knowledge; (2) high interest, low background knowledge; (3) low interest, high background knowledge; and (4) low interest, low background knowledge. The students read a passage and applied their knowledge. As you might guess, the high-interest, high-background-knowledge group performed best. But the high-interest, low-background-knowledge group also did well. It takes both: combination of knowledge and interest.

Teaching for Coherence

Not surprisingly, because there are so many differently wired brains, there are many different ways to create coherence. Any teacher who sticks constantly to only one way of creating coherence will find that a certain subpopulation is consistently not "getting it." Here are three simple teaching strategies that can increase coherence with little effort:

- Select seats that allow students to be able to see the instructor well so that they can take in his or her gestures and facial expressions to get the full effect.
- Use nonverbals, particularly dramatic ones, to have an immediate impact (Nuthall, 1999; Nuthall & Alton-Lee, 1995) as well as a long-term effect on learning (Chesebro, 2003). Dramatic presentations are more memorable (e.g., wearing a special hat or disguise, using a special voice or accent). Vary your tonality or volume to make a special point.
- Use visuals in presentations to increase the impact (Gellevij, Van der Meij, deJong, & Pieters, 2002). Use a mural, a picture, a drawing, or a rough illustration to help students create a mental picture of the new learning (Fiore, Cuevas, Haydee, & Oser, 2003).

Fortunately, you do not have to be over the top to evoke coherence. Simply be aware that you often assume students will understand something easily when in fact they might struggle with it. Instead of blaming the students, walk though the strategies in this book and ask yourself if there are any that you are not currently using.

In addition, you can use six more core strategies to increase coherence: increase key structural knowledge, use experiential learning, use semantic support, use models, add summarizing and discussion, and do elaboration over time. Use these universal strategies at any time. They may not be new to you, but they just may have a new application: coherence.

Over the next several pages, we'll explore these six strategies. Notice how each uses a different set of skills. As you try out each one, you'll notice that one might reach most but not all of your students, and another will reach most, but not all, but it will be a different group of students reached. That's why using several strategies is so critical to successful fierce teaching.

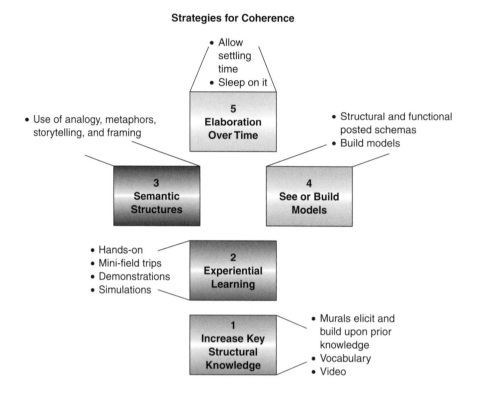

Strategies for Coherence

- Allow settling time
- Sleep on it

5 Elaboration Over Time

- Use of analogy, metaphors, storytelling, and framing

- Structural and functional posted schemas
- Build models

3 Semantic Structures

4 See or Build Models

- Hands-on
- Mini-field trips
- Demonstrations
- Simulations

2 Experiential Learning

1 Increase Key Structural Knowledge

- Murals elicit and build upon prior knowledge
- Vocabulary
- Video

Key Structural Knowledge

Generally, having high background knowledge is a considerable asset in learning. An extensive and growing body of research shows just how much it influences learning. It's valuable because it gives students a springboard of content and process from which they can jump into new material. Students who lack structural knowledge have no safety net and no basis for connection.

McNamara and McDaniel (2004) found that students with high background knowledge were better able to suppress irrelevant or ambiguous information found in poorly written texts, and, in fact, they still learned from them. It's not just the prior knowledge (the content), but also the way that it's known. Hierarchal structures, mental organization, and key concepts provide students with a sense of understanding.

In addition, students could have high prior knowledge, yet be unmotivated to learn new things, so relevance is a critical issue in learning. Lehman and Schraw (2002) found that highly relevant material may compensate for gaps in students' coherence. High relevance provides the motivation and curiosity to dig for or fill in the background knowledge that's missing. The connecting links you provide affect student achievement more than many other variables (S. Snyder, 1993).

Start by building the key process and content features that students need, particularly those with low background knowledge. Start the process years, months, and weeks in advance for maximum benefit. After all, it's unfair to spring brand-new content and brand-new processes on students and hope that they do well.

Practical Suggestions for Increasing Structural Knowledge

- Start with early vocabulary exposure days and weeks before a new unit.
- Use visual tools such as mapping and webbing (Hyerle, 2004).
- Provide brief, skeletal notes before the lecture and the detailed notes afterward (Kiewra, 1985).
- Hold class or small-group discussions.
- Use models.
- Use cooperative, team, or competitive activities that explore students' prior knowledge structures and build on it.
- Provide relevant links to other content and structures.

Experiential Learning

Real-life sensory experiences fill the mind with so much coherent data that there's no classroom comparison. Large, real-life, panoramic visual experiences can provide a cohesive understanding of a concept very quickly. Think of the difference between reading about geology and standing on the edge of the Grand Canyon. That's why going on field trips, conducting indoor or outdoor experiments, watching an event, and seeing someone's body language can all create nearly immediate cohesiveness in the understanding of content. Hands-on science experiments and even outdoor walks on the school campus to explore objects, plants, events, or animals can serve as a mini field trip. Observation, simply watching another person do the task, is effective when followed up by feedback (Zimmerman & Kitsantas, 2002). Adding challenge and social feedback enhances the learning. Clarity is not just an important factor in the student learning experience; it is a make-or-break factor.

Practical Suggestions for Experiential Learning

- Go on indoor or outdoor field trips.
- Conduct experiments inside or outside of class.
- At the high school level, establish business partnerships that allow for learning-to-work opportunities, career preparation, or job training.

Semantic Support

Do some of your friends seem to have a way with words? They may be good at persuasion, evoking images, or storytelling. When they tell a joke or recount yesterday's experiences, the conversation comes alive. This is not a case of charisma, but of using specialized communication tools to provide relevance and coherence.

If there is no perceived relevance, you'll have trouble getting students to care about coherence (Lehman & Schraw, 2002). Generate students' interest by using various semantic support strategies, such as reframing the topic. Stephen Snyder (1991, 1993) found that using semantic devices positively affects student achievement, and achievement is negatively affected by unclear presentations of well-structured, conceptually presented material.

When students use semantic transformations like metaphor or analogy to explain a concept, it shows strong coherence. Teachers often take this kind of knowledge for granted, but they should not. One way to test for coherence is to ask students to create and explain a new definition for a word without using the word itself, such as in the following example:

> Using a metaphor or an analogy, explain any of these concepts below without using the exact same word as listed.
>   energy
>   legal
>   multiply
>   achieve

The ability to do this is a clear indication of a coherent understanding of that word. *Semantic support* means that you'll teach students how to get at the real understanding of a word, idea, or topic by transforming the word into an image, a sound, a feeling, or another way to communicate it through classroom practice.

Practical Suggestions for Semantic Support

- Use analogy ("This microorganism works just like a vacuum cleaner. What does that mean it does?").
- Use metaphors ("The lost dog was searching for its owner. In what ways are we thinking about, caring for, or longing for something of value to us that we miss?").
- Use framing, or put a different spin on something ("Have you ever gotten sore from just sitting? I thought so. Let's take a stretch break.").
- Tell stories ("The strangest thing happened to me last weekend. I was heading out to. . . .").

If you read between the lines, you can see how these could either be done poorly (and in a way that is boring to students) or used to evoke motivation by making the topic more relevant.

The Use of Models

Using models is one of the best ways ever devised to encapsulate learning. Models can be mental models or real-world physical models. The term *mental model,* which refers to internalized representations of a device or an idea held in the mind of one or more persons, has been applied to quite a diverse assembly of representations (Gentner & Stevens, 1983; Johnson-Laird, 1983). DiSessa (1986) describes both *functional* and *structural models:*

- Functional models represent a simple, coherent way to study the selected properties of a system (e.g., an aquarium can provide a model for studying ecosystems). These models illuminate or reveal features or principles about the learning that might never show up in a discussion.
- Structural models provide users with a detailed understanding of a system (e.g., Tinkertoys can demonstrate molecular arrangements).

When students have to make their own models, it shows a deep understanding rarely achievable by more traditional lecture (McLachlan, 2003). Richard Lehrer at the University of Wisconsin at Madison has seen the learning process that happens with the use of models and discusses how first and second graders learn to think differently by having to build a model of an elbow (Penner, Giles, Lehrer, & Schauble, 1997). The kids first used Styrofoam balls and Popsicle sticks. After a discussion about how our flexible elbows work, they changed their approach and used springs and straws. But after more discussion, the children realized that elbows didn't bend 360 degrees, and they came up with a new, even better model. The process of functional model making forced a thoroughness of understanding often unavailable with a textbook. These six-year-olds were doing complex thinking, and the models were the strategy, the feedback, and the product.

Kids who may have low background knowledge or little life experience can benefit greatly when teachers provide coherent models of what's coming up next in class, what's in the teacher's brain.

Practical Suggestions for Using Models

- Post content models in the classroom. Take complex understanding; put it into a simple visual diagram, flow chart, generic formula, pictogram, or visual map; and post it.
- Post processing models for key academic skills (e.g., how to write a summary, how to solve a problem, how to memorize a new concept).
- Post models of key social-emotional skills (e.g., conflict resolution, anger management, making a friend, giving and getting feedback).

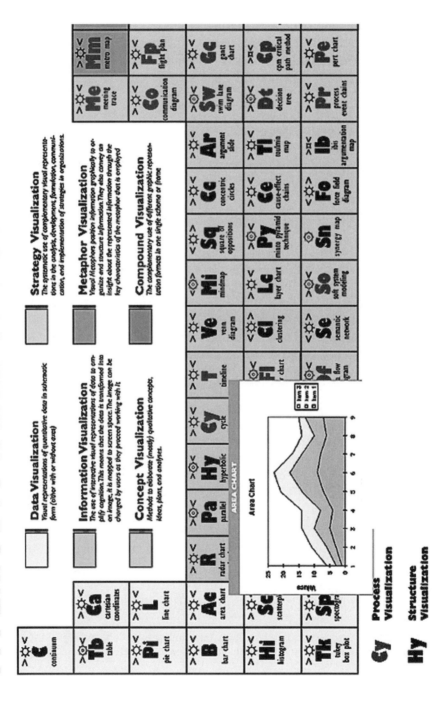

A PERIODIC TABLE OF VISUALIZATION

Data Visualization
Visual representations of quantitative data in schematic form (either with or without axes).

Information Visualization
The use of interactive visual representations of data to amplify cognition. This means that the data is transformed into an image, it is mapped to screen space. The image can be changed by users as they proceed working with it.

Concept Visualization
Methods to elaborate (mostly) qualitative concepts, ideas, plans, and analyses.

Strategy Visualization
The systematic use of complementary visual representations in the analysis, development, formulation, communication, and implementation of strategies in organizations.

Metaphor Visualization
Visual Metaphors position information graphically to organize and structure information. They also convey an insight about the represented information through the key characteristics of the metaphor that is employed.

Compound Visualization
The complementary use of different graphic representation formats in one single schema or frame.

Cy Process Visualization

Hy Structure Visualization

Ask students to redraw any posted model themselves. When they can do it from memory and explain it to another person, you have succeeded.

Summarizing and Discussion

Think of this strategy as *Suped-Up Learning*. This is a tight, concise model that starts with a simple and easy task (word association of known content) and hones it into clear talking points for a fruitful and detailed discussion.

Practical Suggestions for SUPED-Up Learning

- **S:** Students *summarize* what they know so far in one paragraph (five to eight sentences). Before they summarize, either do a whole-group word association brainstorming or allow teams to do it. This will prime the brain for writing. Ensure that students have a model for how to write summary paragraphs (topic sentence, main idea, supporting details, and conclusion).
- **U:** Students *underline* key ideas from the summary and write their questions in the margins. This process teaches critical thinking skills.
- **P:** *Peers* edit what fellow students have written. Students might pass their summary around a circle so that other students can read it quietly and make comments on it, using a class-generated rubric. Or in some classes, students might read a partner's summary and work together to help tighten it up a bit.
- **E:** Students *edit* and revise their original summary based on written or oral feedback to end up with a tighter summary.
- **D:** *Discussion* is held in groups of four to six with a discussion leader and a list of guiding questions.

This is a process that develops many skills used in the digestion, reflection, discussion, writing, and even producing of an artifact of the material after first exposure. The SUPED process, which takes about 45 minutes, nearly guarantees that your students will be able to make sense of the material.

Sleeping on It

It's common that a concept is too new, too complex, or too different to immediately understand and take in deeply. For some students, part of the coherence comes from time. Why? The brain does not easily take big leaps or make paradigm changes. It needs time for new learning to settle in (Blissitt, 2001). Often the hippocampus will hold new learning for days or even weeks before it becomes available for recall. Learners need time to manipulate and digest the material. They need time for the material to fit better in their minds. New ideas are often like new shoes: it takes time for them to feel comfortable.

Practical Suggestions for Sleeping On It

- Use the 51% input time and 49% processing time rule (from Strategy 3, the Input-Output Ratio). This will ensure that students have some time for processing.
- End the lesson with cliffhangers, foreshadowing, or compelling questions to get students' brains curious about what's next. This will also encourage their sub-conscious to process the day's learning.
- Remember that once you have taught 90 percent of your content, take a break from it. Finish the other 10 percent over the next week, even as you start a new section or unit. This allows questions to formulate and meanings to sink in. The last 10 percent of content you save may be what ties much of it together.

SUMMARY

Many students nod their heads in agreement as they are learning, but that's not necessarily coherence. Keep experimenting with different ways to ensure that everyone gets the content in his or her own way. The fierce teacher may use three to five different strategies in each unit to ensure coherence. Do not expect students to get complex learning the first time through, even when it's coherent—that's only going to be surface learning. This is not a bad thing (initially), but a reminder that it takes many layers—visuals, elaborations, vocabulary work, models, framing—to develop the understanding of complexity with some coherence. In some cases, it's simply a matter of time (Wilson, 2002). Learners might just need to sleep on it. The fierce teacher understands that coherence is in the top seven of all learning factors and makes it a priority every day.

Strategy 7

Environmental Management

THE FOUR ENVIRONMENTAL DOMAINS

Environments either impair or support the learner. There is no neutral environment. This strategy focuses on the four environmental domains in which all student learning takes place: cultural, physical, academic, and social. A researcher might conduct a study on which type of strategy works best, but what also matters may be the room temperature, the students' relationship with the teacher, the amount of lighting available, or even the ethnic background of the teacher. There is no context-free learning (Sternberg & Grigorenko, 2001). We are always in some kind of environment, and even the lack of richness in an environment creates some kind of a context, even if it's a negative one. Nature, it seems, abhors a vacuum and always fills space with something. The fierce teacher is one who actively manages the environment to orchestrate student success.

The principle of environment management states that environment plays a key role in any student's performance. It asserts, with scientific evidence, that you cannot measure a student in isolation—although it's supposedly done all the time. The school environment influences students so much that the four environmental domains become make-or-break factors in determining students' likelihood to succeed or fail. The sheer amount of time that we expect students to be in school (from K through Grade 12, it's over 13,000 hours) is both a huge opportunity and a huge responsibility. If you thought that school was merely about "filling the vessel" with information, you might want to think again. New evidence states that the environments we establish may be doing more than helping students feel comfortable or not. Our environments may be strongly influencing the developing brain via the following:

- the growth and survival (or stunting) of brand-new brain cells
- the present-time alteration of genes (accidental and purposeful mutants)
- enabling the brain to recover from environmental toxins, aggression, disease, substance abuse, trauma, and learning disabilities
- affecting cognitive capacity and emotional responsiveness

Neuroscientist John Cairns's blockbuster work shows that genes are not set for life. His studies used bacteria, but nonetheless, the results were astonishing. When deprived of their normal food sources, under severe stress the bacteria actively rewrote their own genes to alter and adapt them to environmental signals coming from the highly stressful environment (Cairns, Overbaugh, & Miller, 1988). The adapted genes, now a purposeful mutation, activated proteins, which activated brand-new behaviors that enabled the bacteria to survive. The mutations were not random; rather, a stressful test tube environment altered them. This classic experiment was recently verified (Appenzeller, 1999; Balter, 2000).

Epigenetic (*"outside of the gene"*) refers to the capacity of genes to respond to environmental signals such as stress, activity, and emotions. The significance of this is profound: environments can and do have a far more powerful impact than earlier thought (Heindel, McAllister, Worth, & Tyson, 2006). While you don't see the effects over a single hour or day, it adds up. Environments can have a significant, life-changing impact on our students (Lipton, 2005; Rossi, 2002).

Epigenetic influences can happen within minutes, but more typically they happen with acute or chronic input. The greater the contrast with an alternative setting and the greater the consistency in any environment, the more likely any organism will adapt to it. In terms of human studies, carefully designed long-term research has used data from adoption of children with low IQs into healthy two-parent homes. In one study of children adopted after four years of age, they had an average IQ gain of 13.9 points eight years after adoption and an astonishing 19.5 points when they were adopted by high-socioeconomic-status families (Duyme, Dumaret, & Tomkiewicz, 1999). Any teacher who thinks that "slower" kids are stuck the way they are is not paying attention to the research. Environments change the brain!

How, specifically, can your school environments change your students? The environments affect the well-being, stress levels, confidence, safety, and access to information, and certainly modulate relationships and ultimately influence our values. In other words, they have a great deal to do with how our students turn out. Most teachers know the power of a well-designed classroom, and they invest time before school starts to get the physical classroom just right. Yet some teachers drop the ball after that.

Manage the stress or they'll achieve less

They fail to understand the power of well-managed environments and leave most of it to chance. Big mistake. Let's get started with managing the physical environment.

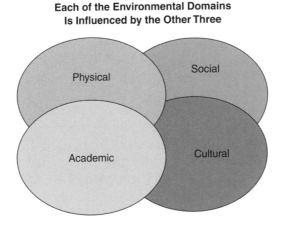

Each of the Environmental Domains Is Influenced by the Other Three

The Physical Environment

As humans, we are quite aware of the physical environment in which we live and work, and that it has a profound effect on us. Chances are, your environment means a great deal to you. The emerging paradigm is that physical environments can physically change the brain, and those changes may have far-reaching effects on learning, health, cognition, and behavior. Although it's difficult to quantify the overall effect, several researchers have found a profound influence (e.g., Moore & Lackney, 1993; Schneider, 2002). At the low end, estimates place the effects of the physical school environment on student success as low as 1 to 3 percent, yet it may well be 40 to 50 percent or more at the upper end.

How Do Environments Affect Us?

Our sensory awareness provides the perception about our environments. Awareness means that the sensory input proceeds to your "sensory antenna," which is located on the outside of skin cells that make contact with the environment. In addition, our other sensory receptors (e.g., eyes, ears, nose, tongue) take in extensive amounts of sensory information. When any suboptimal change takes place in our environment, a signal from our receptors sends the message to our effectors (change agents) also located on our skin cells (Hagmann, 1999). This message activates a change of behavior in our proteins (e.g., shiver, sweat, run). Our sensitivity is nonstop. In fact, Jeffrey Lackney (1994) at the University of Wisconsin at Madison found that the physical facility is a core factor in learning—it affects lighting, student safety, visibility, heating and cooling, and instructional opportunities. Every dollar spent on better-quality school environments is returned in better student achievement for the life of the school. In some cases, there's a return for 30 years!

Indoor air quality. The U.S. General Accounting Office (1995) has studied indoor air quality (IAQ) and found 15,000 schools have bad IAQ. That's 8 million children, or 1 in 5 children in America's schools (Lemasters, 1997, later verified this finding). The symptoms of bad IAQ include irritated eyes, nose, and throat; upper respiratory infections; nausea; dizziness; headaches and fatigue; and sleepiness—all of which add up to a recipe for poor learning. In fact, they fit perfectly the Environmental Protection Agency's (2000) designation for *sick building syndrome.*

Acoustic quality. Environmental noise, like sounds from traffic, trains, and airplanes, disturbs learning. This topic has been well studied because, for instance, it is easy to find schools in a flight path. Evans and Maxwell (1999) examined 100 random student groups enrolled in two New York City schools; one group was in the flight path of an airport, and the other was not. The students exposed to the air-traffic noise scored as much as 20 percent lower on a reading test than the students in the other school.

Inside the classroom, noisy heaters and air conditioners are the biggest source of noise (Feth, 1999), and both can drive students and teachers crazy. Poor acoustical conditions often negatively impact students with normal hearing (Nelson & Soli, 2000; Smaldino & Crandell, 2000). And it has been found that the inclusion of sound-absorbing material in a classroom to mask ambient noise dramatically improves students' speech discrimination (Pekkarinen & Wiljanen, 1990). The optimal solution is to install in every classroom a sound system that has speakers in the ceiling and a wireless microphone for the teacher to use; this setup reduces teacher stress and improves student performance (Jonsdottir, Laukkanen, & Siikki, 2003; Mendel, Roberts, & Walton, 2003). The fierce teacher is on a mission to get the big three (temperature, acoustics, and lighting) in the best possible condition.

Classroom lighting. A Department of Education study from Alberta, Canada, showed that students enrolled in schools with above-average lighting had higher attendance, higher physical growth rates, increased concentration, and better academic performance (Hathaway, 1992). Schools' electricity requirements are so great that the real cost-savings may be in building skylights and even installing solar panels. But the evidence is strong against low-light days for students. Keep the classrooms bright and find other areas to cut costs.

The Heschong Mahone Group has conducted several major studies on lighting. It was found that students with the most sunlight in their classrooms progressed up to 20 percent faster on state standardized math tests and 26 percent faster on reading tests, compared to students in classrooms with the least lighting (Heschong Mahone Group, 1999). These gains are astonishing, considering how hard school districts try to raise reading and math scores. Lighting alone influences standardized reading and math scores by as much as 15 to 25 percent (Heschong Mahone Group, 2008).

Classroom temperature. Research has shown that an increasing number of environmental variables can influence cognition. For example, reading comprehension declines when room temperature rises above 74 degrees Fahrenheit, while math skills decline when it gets above 77 degrees (Lackney, 1994). Professor Alan Hedge at Cornell University found that when temperatures get too cool (in the 60s), typing mistakes go up by 74 percent and typing speed drops by 46 percent, compared to when temperatures are in the 70s. We can all adjust to a room that is 5 degrees too cold or too hot, but classrooms that are kept between 68 and 72 degrees are most comfortable for the majority of students.

School administrators who think they're saving money by not using air conditioners are fooling themselves; they'll end up spending more money on other ways to improve student achievement. Considering all the money spent on student achievement, here's another fierce strategy: give teachers control over their own classrooms. Teachers with the ability to control their classroom's temperature have students who achieve higher

(Heschong Mahone Group, 1999). It's not just the feeling of empowerment for the teacher; it's that a teacher right there, in the room, can account for and make a decision. When there's glare, heat waves, dampness, or temporary changes, a savvy teacher can adjust on the spot. Teachers are held accountable for student performance, so it makes sense that they should be given the authority to influence the environment in which they and the students do their work. Removing such simple decision-making authority from teachers handicaps them.

There are many other variables that influence the physical environment. For example, simple things like the view outside the windows or the posters on the walls can influence student learning. Having clear air and the right humidity level can help as well. And in a perfect world, we would have enough elbowroom in class so that students do not feel so crowded; overcrowding inevitably creates stress. But the primary message here is this: the physical environment matters so much to student achievement that to ignore it is irresponsible.

Top 10 Variables:
in Your Environment

1. Humidity moderate and water available
2. Optimal acoustics for listening
3. Colorful walls, positive colors
4. Temperature at 66–74F (20–23C)
5. Flexible seating with options
6. Aesthetics: calming distant view
7. Teacher control of heat and light
8. Learner safety/No threats
9. 30–35 sq. ft. of class space per student
10. Bright, well-lit (no glare) classrooms

The Social Environment

Traditional educators think of learning as an individual act, but that logic doesn't add up. Students spend over 2,300 days (13 years at 180 days per year) from kindergarten through 12th grade in a primarily social context. They are in lines, teams, classes, clubs, cliques, grade-level groups, and schools. The school's social context has a profound effect on the developing brain. Humans develop in a social world that shapes, sculpts, and changes the growing brain in dramatic new ways that no one suspected for a long time. A burgeoning new field, social neuroscience, has revealed an astonishing array of multilevel influences that social contact has on the brain. All of us see it in a school setting; we see the influence of solitude, the power of gangs, and the effects of a smile, a touch, and even a sarcastic remark.

Social Influences on Our Brains, Bodies, and Lives

Social conditions influence or involve nearly every system in the human body. A systems analysis suggests that events at one level of an organism (e.g., molecular, DNA, cellular, nervous system, organs, immune, behavioral, social) can profoundly influence events at other levels (Cacioppo, Berntson, Sheridan, & McClintock, 2001). A social event is not isolated from the rest of the mind and body—and we ought to pay closer attention to the effects of social contacts at school. On the short list, we might include the following:

- learning and cognition
- memory and recall
- addiction and reward
- perception and judgment
- stress and trauma
- immunity and health
- responses to drugs

Nobel Laureate Eric Kandel has shown that social contact influences gene expression. This profound new understanding moves far beyond the old paradigm of social influence as incidental. "We now know the subjective experiences of human consciousness, our perception of free will, behavior, and social dynamics can modulate gene expression, and vice versa" (Kandel, 1998). Your school's social environment has a significant effect on your students; it affects gene expression. Healthy social contact improves immune activity, and social stress weakens immune systems (Padgett et al., 1998; Padgett & Sheridan, 1999). In fact, social isolation is as devastating a risk factor as smoking or high blood pressure (Harlow & Harlow, 1973; House, Landis, & Umberson, 1988). A single threatening situation may alter behavior indefinitely (Wiedenmayer, 2004).

Another interesting biological phenomenon is the influence that social status has on serotonin levels (Summers et al., 2004). Serotonin is an important neurotransmitter in the brain, and moderate levels are highly implicated with attention, mood, and memory (Huang, Tsai, & Chang, 2004), all of which can drive achievement. In addition, lower serotonin levels are correlated with inflexible behaviors (Clarke, Dalley, Crofts, Robbins, & Roberts, 2004).

Social status, serotonin, and academic achievement are all correlated. The higher the social status, the more protection one has against fluctuations of serotonin and stressful situations (Manuck, Flory, Ferrell, & Muldoon, 2004). Helping students achieve high social status can serve as a protective mechanism for overall health. In fact, studies have shown that social rejection is so bad for us that it activates the same place in the brain that real physical pain activates (Eisenberger, Jarcho, Lieberman, & Naliboff, 2006; Panksepp, 2003).

Positive Social Structures Work Miracles

Improving the sense of community at school can translate to higher test scores (Gregoire, Ashton, & Algina, 2004). Many types of social structures at school can help you do just that. There are less structured models (e.g., context-dependent friendships, a temporary class partner for an activity) and more structured models (e.g., ability grouping, cooperative learning groups). Cooperative learning pioneers Roger and David Johnson (1999) have a distinct model for cooperative learning, which defines one of the key elements as *positive interdependency.*

The perception among those using cooperative social support is that academic challenges are more achievable (Ghaith, 2002). Students achieve more even if the increase is not always robust, and other social values also are typically improved (Gillies & Ashman, 1998). Positive time with established peers can reduce stress, and for many, learning in groups reduces stress. Research suggests that quality cooperative learning programs produce better learning when compared to programs in which students compete against each other individually (Lipsey & Wilson, 1993; Walberg, 1999). Positive social supports boost students' self-esteem and create hope and optimism, which influence brain chemistry and capability assessments.

Independent Learners

What about students who don't like working in groups? Listen to these students, of course, but also provide some variety in groupings and choice. We should respect, but not necessarily cave in to, their wishes. It's still important to (1) explain why we are asking them to do something they don't wish to and (2) provide some variety so that no student has to spend 100 percent of his or her time in an uncomfortable, stressful social structure. Encourage students to expand their comfort zones. One study among sixth graders randomly assigned them to work either in triads or individually on computer-based problems (Barron, 2000). After the initial assignment grouping was over, the students who had worked in triads outperformed (as individuals) the students who had not worked in cooperative groups.

Classroom Dialogues to Build Social Structures

Beginning in elementary school, teachers should hold forthright and practical discussions on class rules, racism, classroom bullying, cliques, and responding to a disaster in a foreign country. We should increase the variety and frequency of discussions and even social gatherings. Foster thoughtful deliberations among students, with clear rules such as no put-downs, listening to others' points of view, and learning to argue with evidence, not against the person. Teachers can model and insist on open and real deliberation, even at the primary level. Education professor Walter Parker (2005) suggests that it's important to do the following:

- choose topics meaningful to the children
- ensure diversity in the contributors
- keep the discussion free from domination
- ensure that the teacher is skilled in open dialogue techniques
- focus on having a better understanding of our actions

At the secondary level, Power, Higgins, and Kohlberg (1989) have developed curriculum models that change the whole social culture at schools. These models show that engaging students in creating a better social and democratic climate can be highly empowering. Students begin to see school as much more like the real world, where they have a genuine say in things.

Social Status Strategies in Motion

Let's start with a fundamental rule: orchestrate the way kids socialize. Do not leave student socialization to chance; it is a learned skill and one that needs ongoing attention and development. Here are some suggestions for fostering socialization:

- In Portland, Oregon, a physical education teacher teaches school staff how to do their own daily assemblies that build physical, emotional, and social skills. Typically, these rituals take just 15 to 20 minutes and take the form of a start-the-day rev-up assembly for the entire school.
- Students enjoy having a home "base group" or "family" for the daily or weekly routine and for comfort. At the secondary level, this can be the group they meet in to start the day, and at the primary level, they can both start and end the day in this group. This social group should provide a dependable initial structure for engaging in academics.
- Make every student a part of a club, friendship, team, or group. At the elementary and primary levels, small classes or cooperative learning groups (usually four students) may be the most appropriate social structure. At the high school and college levels, use varied structures like project teams, pairs, or triads. Pair every student at school with another student or an adult who is their official mentor.
- Keeping children together with a particular teacher for two or more years (often referred to as *looping*) can build relationships between learners and caring adults if the teachers have the appropriate skills.
- Help children and teens feel important every day. Greet them at the door, recognize birthdays, honor their answers (right or wrong), share student leadership and responsibilities, discover the gifts in every student, and use affirmations every day.

As you work on school or classroom social strategies, never expect all social groupings to magically work well on their own. Humans have differences, which can create stress and conflict. Allow time and resources for group maintenance. Social structures take time to nurture and develop. Fierce teaching means being proactive in managing the social climate.

The Academic Environment

The climate created by peers, school staff, the curriculum, and each classroom teacher speaks volumes about the excitement, relevance, and appropriateness of the school curriculum. Implicit and explicit messages about the curriculum play a significant role in the academic achievement of students. The academic climate is the aggregate of all the value-carrying messages students receive over time at school. The fierce teacher actively manages the academic climate to ensure student success.

For most educators, the academic climate is what emerges at their school over time. Many see it as a lucky or random result of characteristics of the school, the teachers, and the students. To the fierce teacher, it is actually the result of a carefully orchestrated campaign to generate strong positive values about the relevance and positive emotions of a good education. The academic climate ought to carry the students in your classroom, like the invisible cables that make Broadway stage characters from Peter Pan appear to fly.

The Five Success Factors

How do schools create an academic climate that fosters learning? There are five success factors for accomplishing a strong, positive academic climate:

- celebrate and affirm the learning
- life-path guidance
- the use of traditions
- instructional variety
- student asset building

Celebrate and Affirm the Learning. There is nothing hardwired into a student's brain that says, "It's better to get good grades than poor ones." There's no genetic instruction to work hard in school or be thorough and accurate in homework assignments. This means that it is absolutely mandatory to have schoolwide celebrations to appreciate staff members who are engaged in lifelong learning (getting advanced degrees) and students who deserve extra recognition, and to acknowledge the entire school when benchmarks are met. Genuine celebrations create positive emotions that become associated with achievement.

Life-Path Guidance. Students will become more vested academically if they see a future in it. It is up to the adults in their lives to slowly develop a set of values and challenging curriculum that includes succeeding in school, whether it's high school or a career or technical-vocational school. For many students, often those most at risk for dropping out, vocational pathways are a lifeline. High school students who are engaged in work experiences, apprenticeships, or service learning are likely to attain higher GPAs in their freshman year of college than those with no such experiences in high school (U.S. Department of Education, 2004).

What about curriculum for those students who don't see college in their future? Keep in mind that IQ is not the most important factor for getting into and attending college. Research has shown that IQ is variable and can be raised as much as 20 points (Jensen, 2006). Never assume that kids are not cut out for college. For example, Preuss secondary school in San Diego exposes students to a challenging college prep curriculum. Each year, over 90 percent of these students go on to a four-year university in spite of the fact that 100 percent of them receive free and reduced lunch and are from families that meet the federal guidelines for poverty. Life-path guidance means offering all possibilities to all students and requiring that every student has a mandatory meeting with a school counselor.

The Use of Traditions. Traditions (or classroom rituals) are orchestrated events within a culture that serve recurring needs. Outside of school, traditions include birthdays, weddings, holidays, anniversaries, and homecomings. Within schools, many strong traditions are more sports related than academics related. While most of us recognize the value of sports, relying too heavily on sports traditions could send the message to students that academics are just "something we need to get through." This is often a case of low expectations. Increase the quantity of academic traditions, and increase the number of people who participate in those traditions. Your school's goal ought to be "Let's make learning more cool than not learning, and let's do it for every student at school." Whereas all teachers have daily procedures, rituals and traditions are orchestrated as a class in order to create a sense of community and always end things on a positive note. For example, you could put every student into a team, and the teams could compete in academic marathons that last through each unit, all year long. In the end, these peers would vote on different levels of recognition for each team's performance.

Instructional Variety. One way to virtually guarantee that most students will succeed is by using a wide range of instructional strategies. We educators can all become creatures of habit, but why not ask 81,000 kids from 110 high schools what instructional strategies they learn from best (Yazzie-Mintz, 2006)? The top three are discussion and debate, group projects, and art and drama activities. What was their least favorite? Lecture—and it was the strategy of choice for most teachers. But getting some teachers to stray from their favorite strategy is challenging. Listen to the kids; if you want them to be excited about academics, use the strategies they learn from best.

Student Asset Building. Students bring a particular package of cultural, academic, emotional, and strategic assets to school. In a perfect world, this package would always be enough for success, but that's not often the case. It's up to you to figure out what students bring to the table and whether that'll be enough to succeed in your class. You can increase the assets of your students by the priorities you make and the resulting choices you follow. The greater number of and quality of student assets, the greater the capacity. We all know that there's more to learning than just the capacity factor. But without it, learning isn't likely to happen. Students' will and motivation drive their success and their focus on academics.

If you want to improve on student assets, focus on these: reading skills, study skills, metaskills, social-emotional skills, goal setting, attitude management, and deferred gratification. If you even suspect that a student is struggling with reading, please do three things. Talk to the student privately and (a) tell him or her that it's not an indicator of IQ or effort, (b) get the student some help, and (c) provide long-term support for him or her. Study skills and metaskills (thinking about thinking) are the factors that are most related to achievement among college students (Onwuegbuzie, Slate, Paterson, Watson, & Schwartz, 2000). Better study skills help students learn better, and the more content one knows, the greater the likelihood for using metacognitive strategies. Social-emotional skills develop through strong community building and cooperative learning activities. To encourage goal setting, attitude management, and deferred gratification, help students set big goals with shorter, manageable microgoals. Celebrate the little successes, and keep up the positive support on the path to greater, more time-consuming goals. Allow students to struggle a bit, and encourage them to work through the frustration of long-term gratification.

There's no one thing you do that will magically create a positive academic climate; it's the aggregate of what you do over time. If you made a list from this section of five ideas that you could implement, do just one per month, continuing the current one into the next month when you start a new one. Over time, you'll be doing multiple things simultaneously and getting the climate (and results) you want.

The Cultural Environment

Traditionally, educators though it was genes and parenting that influenced school-age behaviors. But culture influences teacher behavior and student achievement. In *The Nurture Assumption*, Judith Harris (1998) argues that it is peers (the social environment) who affect behavior the most. Parents have little direct (only indirect) effects on academic and social outcomes. Most likely, you've felt, seen, and heard the impact of culture on your own behavior, so it stands to reason that classroom culture can and does affect student achievement as well (Hirschy & Wilson, 2002).

We could group or classify the culture that schools created in many ways, but we'll focus on just three of them: the culture of success, the culture of character, and the culture of respect.

The Culture of Success Is All About Achievement

Each student's culture exerts a strong influence in terms of the values communicated through family, neighborhood, and social events. Parents often prioritize the focus of their kids through their types of support (Steinberg, Dornbusch, & Brown, 1992). For example, among many Hispanics, family cohesiveness and support is more valued than academic success. Among many Asian immigrants, effort expended is more important than talent or ability. In Asian cultures, adolescents often feel more parental pressure to succeed through effort (Chen & Lan, 1998), and they tend to want to please their parents more than their Caucasian counterparts do.

The Counterculture of Success Is That of Disengagement From the System

Typically, students will either find other ways to feel like they are "winning" (e.g., hobbies, athletics, video games) or find evidence that winning isn't all it's cracked up to be anyway (e.g., gangs, apathy). An early casualty of this counterculture is learning. Students may develop learned helplessness or simply lose interest in learning because they've decided that they can't win academically. Many students choose not to become a success because they perceive the barriers as too high or they do not feel they have the support (Kenny, Blustein, Chaves, Grossman, & Gallagher, 2003). Studies show that both Hispanics and African-Americans suffer from a lack of peer support for success, which creates a strong negative factor for likely achievement and may be mitigated by a stronger school climate (Steinberg et al., 1992). This suggests that having discussions with students about their perceptions of the barriers and brainstorming solutions and action plans may be a good starting point for putting students on the road to success.

The Culture of Character Values Responsibility, Honesty, and Fairness

It also supports the essentials of emotional intelligence, which include knowing oneself, empathy, and listening skills. Schools that place value on positive character often reach out to create learning communities with the mantra of "We all can and do make a difference." Research tells us that high school peer group characteristics affect grade point average (Betts & Morell, 1999). The culture of character, not surprisingly, places strong emphasis on character education. It typically starts in a morning homeroom, and teachers are encouraged to integrate mini lessons on positive qualities throughout the day.

The Counterculture to Character Is Rebellion

The rebel is likely to be a contrarian or a discipline problem, involved in violence, deviance, and other rule-breaking activities. Here there are many losses; one of the first is safety, and that means learning and certainly strong achievement is impaired. Evidence suggests that being male and doing poorly in school are the two greatest risk factors for deviant behavior (Davies, 1999). Case and Katz (1991) have shown significant peer effects on youth criminal behavior and drug use. When schools have a culture of violence, it affects different populations differently. Among African American adolescent males, exposure to violence and victimization is strongly associated with delinquency, while adolescent females often show symptoms of posttraumatic stress disorder.

The Culture of Respect Acknowledges That You Are Somebody

Subcultures of perceived nobodies in the past have included anyone who is in the "out" group, special needs learners, and even those from out of town. We are more likely to respect those who are just like us. Those who are different—from the teachers, from other students—find it harder to fit in. Respect means that there is an attitude of admiration and deference to or equality with others. This is a serious issue because 80 percent of teachers say they feel unprepared to teach and reach diverse populations (Futrell, Gomez, & Bedden, 2003). The fierce teacher helps students find what they have in common with each other and still honor differences.

The Counterculture Exists Where Students Disrespect Others

In this culture you have prejudice, bullying, name-calling, put-downs, exclusionary tactics, bias, and even hate crimes. Learning cannot thrive in a climate where your dignity, safety, and reputation are under constant fire. The research tells us that a strong ethnic identity and bicultural self-efficacy can be best thought of as protective factors against youth violence. A culture that fosters positive ethnic identity and self-esteem contributes to young people's perceptions of their ability to achieve academically (E. Smith, Walker, Fields, Brookins, & Seay, 1999). Classroom teachers can influence student expectancy and goals through skill building, optimism, and positive comments about students.

Building Positive Cultures

Make extra efforts to support hiring practices that promote diversity. There is some, but not conclusive, evidence that students do better in classes and at schools where they see and interact with those of their same race (Dee, 2004). At your school, show your support of diversity. This means not just in hiring, but whom you show in pictures, whom you talk about, and whom you use as examples. Students notice a mentor as a good or bad example to follow.

Kids at most schools hear slurs on a daily basis. School bullying has increased over the past 10 years. In fact, up to 8 percent of students report

www.jensenlearning.com

that they have been bullied in the past six months (National Center for Education Statistics, 2003). Take the time at your school to address bullying, poor school culture, and threats of all kinds. When you remove the threats that reinforce stereotypes, those students who had been disadvantaged will perform better on standardized tests (Gooda, Aronson, & Inzlicht, 2003).

Practical Suggestions on Promoting School Culture

Perspectives, a new charter school in Chicago, made school culture its focus. Its theme is "A Disciplined Life." And although the school is not perfect, students thrive in this climate, even if they had only experienced failure before (Schulla-Cose & Day, 2004). The school simply made culture a priority, and the climate supported the learning. Perspectives has found that relationships, dialogue, and communications skills lead to better student achievement. Here are some suggestions for promoting positive school culture:

- There is already a culture in place, even though it may not be the one you want. Start by doing your homework and discovering the real unseen or quiet culture

(Continued)

(Continued)

in your school (D'Alessandra & Devyani Sadhal, 1998). There are even surveys that do this (e.g., School Culture Scale); the Character Education Partnership (2005) indexes many such surveys and scales and provides ratings on (1) administration and scoring, (2) reliability, and (3) validity. If you examine this index, pay particular attention to the scales with an aggregate score of six or higher on all these variables. Once you know the culture, you can design a plan that incorporates the reality of the existing paradigm. Be sure to include a research-based or well-proven model. Even among the most disadvantaged students, having a working model is essential (Tucker & Herman, 2002).

- Honor differences, and allow for unique approaches. Make sure that students understand there are many ways to be smart and to make it in this world. Evidence is strong that IQ is just one of many types of intelligence (Sternberg, 2003). Integrate programs into the rest of the curriculum, school operations, and accountability practices (Greenberg et al., 2003). Make sure all teachers understand and use differentiation strategies.

- Support teachers in developing students' help-seeking skills and the confidence to actually use those behaviors in the classroom (Newman, 2000). Helplessness is in contrast to being assertive in getting what you need to achieve. Support class discussions on stereotype and race issues. Among African Americans, 47 percent found such discussions helpful, and over a third of Anglos and 54 percent of Hispanics found them somewhat or greatly helpful (Richard, 2004).

- Be more assertive in establishing a climate of tolerance. A superb resource for both teachers and students is the Southern Poverty Law Center's (n.d.) *101 Tools for Tolerance*. New teachers should have training in conflict resolution, reading emotional states, and developing empathy skills. New teachers usually don't have these skills (Mendes, 2002). Empathy is critical because many students come from high-stress backgrounds that make positive behavior at school more difficult (McGee et al., 2001). Watch out for the negative effects of slurs, bullying, or other acts of disrespect (Wessler, 2004). If you try to ignore the problem or maybe just deal with the symptoms, you practically guarantee not only that the problem will reoccur, but that students will underachieve academically.

- Use schoolwide activities that include and involve all students in events that unify. Some sports teams accomplish this feeling; for other schools, partnering with parents, businesses, or community resources can make things happen. You will need to create your own rituals and special events, which should have the following characteristics:
  o include all grades (full participation, with staff)
  o include many people (including student leaders) in the planning process
  o long-term focus (use of constant rituals)
  o establish high expectations for success

School cultures exist everywhere we go. They will develop even if you do nothing. But there is an accumulating body of evidence that school culture is a significant influence on emotional, social, and academic success. You can choose to either ignore it and pay the price or be proactive and reap the benefits. First, assess your own classroom or school climate. Next, create a list of the potential strategies you can use. Make a goal of implementation (e.g., you'll do one strategy per month). Finally, make it a fierce teacher habit to continue to strengthen and monitor the environment until you get it where you want it. The beauty of this is that environments can be so powerful, so positive, and so encompassing that a good one almost teaches the students for you.

SUMMARY

The four environmental domains in which all student learning takes place are cultural, physical, academic, and social. We could argue about which matters most—the teacher's skill level, character, content knowledge, personality—but we can all agree that the environment in which we work plays a key part in the process of learning. The message here is that you do have influence over the environment you create and that influence is a critical ingredient in the success of your students.

Epilogue

MAKING FIERCE TEACHING HAPPEN

The focus in education everywhere is on student achievement. Earlier I said (and supported with research) that the single most reliable way to boost student achievement is through quality teaching and quality, sustained staff development. When done well, these can mitigate the effects of many other factors, such as low socioeconomic status, lack of school resources, and having staff who are too inexperienced or who are going to retire soon. But what about getting staff to make these real-world changes in their behavior?

MAKING THE CHOICE FOR CHANGE

As you know, change is not easy for most of us. Dr. Edward Miller, dean of the medical school at Johns Hopkins University, says that given a choice between changing lifestyle and an increased risking of dying, 90 percent of coronary bypass patients won't make the change (Deutschman, 2005). Is it any better at your school? If you were an administrator, what could you do to make changes that haven't already been tried? Maybe some of these sound attractive to you:

- **Increase the pressure:** Add high-stakes testing to put more pressure on students. This assumes that motivation is a persistent issue. There are some who respond positively to this approach, but not everyone.
- **Give maximum choice to staff and students regarding what and how to learn**: This idea assumes that you already have highly motivated students and they only need to pick the appropriate match for their present levels.
- **Improve the use of differentiation, multiple intelligences, and learning styles:** This strategy assumes that you have a highly

talented staff with great execution skills who already know (and use) the material in this book.

- **Add more pullout and acceleration programs:** This assumes that you have the resources, the special education staff, the gifted and talented staff, and the extracurricular options. This is an excellent idea as long as your staff already knows (and uses) the fundamentals outlined in this book.
- **Use screen testing to match students with staff, school, and curriculum:** This is an option for private and some charter schools, but not public ones. At most schools, there is little choice when it comes to the "raw materials."
- **Threaten teachers if their students don't get high scores:** Publish each classroom's scores in the paper, list teachers' names, and threaten not to renew their contracts if the scores don't improve.
- **Jump on bandwagons:** Try every score-raising, test-prep program around. The main objective here is to look good and save your job while abandoning the pursuit of developing good human beings who value each other and love learning.

Motivation to Get Started

If these options don't appeal to you, keep reading. They haven't been very attractive to others, either. The ideal motivation comes from within. Yet what else can you do? As I mentioned early in the book, the evidence is pretty solid that improving the quality of teachers is the single most researched, most likely, most reliable way to improve student achievement. You can either become one of the significant players in education who make a stand for what's good, right, and important about education or you can become like those who feel that they've "lost their soul" in teaching. Reconnect with the experience of doing what matters most in teaching. By doing that, you'll get the maximum return on your efforts.

People make personal changes because of a compelling and emotional story, theme, or hook than for any other reason. If you want your staff to get on board, bring in a student with a before-and-after story who can talk to your staff about how a teacher using certain methods kept him or her in school. A relevant, compelling, and emotional story will get more people on board than any other strategy. Another example of a compelling story is that some schools create an "us against the rest of the district/world (or anyone else who doesn't believe in us)" mentality. This gets all the staff to rally collectively around a cause.

Gather Data

Before you jump in and decide which of this book's sections, chapters, or strategies you want to take action on, let's step back for a moment and gather data. Use your collected data to help pinpoint where this book can interface in your staff development. Integrate this book with clear, regular, and useful data about your students. Evidence suggests that when teachers get clear, current, and useful data (not the finger-pointing or threatening type), they are willing to make changes. Research also suggests that more frequent feedback, along with staff development and school climate support, can and does improve student achievement (Phillips, Fuchs, & Fuchs, 1994).

But let's consider the big picture and how each of us can play a part in change. Everyone can do something, and what you do may depend on the motivation, resources, and power at your disposal. Much of the decision depends on your role. None of the roles listed here are mutually exclusive, but you should have a primary affiliation.

Make a Plan

Principals, vice principals, and superintendents can effect changes by sharing a clear, coherent vision of hope; reducing bureaucracy for staff; getting funding to support better staff development; visiting classrooms and complimenting teachers; being a steady hand and dependable listener; and taking good care of those on the front lines—the teachers. Solve teacher issues such as stress, lack of time, collegiality, and quality training. When you put teachers in the number-one position, they'll put kids first because, when supported, teachers typically love to put kids first. Allow opportunities for teachers to do the following:

- develop more useful schoolwide collaborative assessment tools with their students
- watch staff-to-staff conversations—stick to positives
- brainstorm with other staff members and follow up on the ideas they develop
- provide quality staff development
- help each other begin study groups with this book

Pick just one of the following core factors to begin with; these drive successful learning more than anything else. To help you recall them, use the acronym **Be Fierce**:

BE—body and emotional connections

F—feedback and error correction

I—input-to-output ratio

E—elaboration for depth

R—recall and memory management

C—content coherence

E—environmental management

Jump Right In

Teachers play a huge role in how their students turn out. Always talk about your students as "our kids" not "those kids." Doing nothing will ensure more of the same, if not worse. At your school, you can do the following:

- work first on the seven core strategies for learning presented in this book
- set manageable monthly goals, and stick to them
- make one small change per week, and practice it until it's second nature
- make a big change each month, and practice it until you're good at it
- celebrate progress, and set new goals

SUMMARY

If you are reading this book, you're a player in this large game called education. But the game is real, and lives are at stake. You have the power to read, to learn, and to take action. Find the part you can play with purpose and passion. Your students, your school, the community, and your conscience are waiting. The fierce teacher makes a decision to believe and a decision to take action. What do you believe, and what will you do?

References

Aksoya, T., & Link, C. (2000). A panel analysis of student mathematics achievement in the U.S. in the 1990s: Does increasing the amount of time in learning activities affect math achievement? *Economics of Education Review, 19,* 261–277.

Als, H., Duffy, F., McAnulty, G., Rivkin, M., Vajapeyam, S., Mulkern, R., et al. (2004). Early experience alters brain function and structure. *Pediatrics, 113,* 846–857.

Altmann, G. (2003). Learning and development in neural networks—The importance of prior experience. *Cognition, 88,* 171–199.

Appenzeller, T. (1999). Test tube evolution catches time in a bottle. *Science, 284,* 2108–2110.

Ashby, F. G., Isen, A. M., & Turken, A. U. (1999). A neuropsychological theory of positive affect and its influence on cognition. *Psychological Review, 106,* 529–550.

Assor, A., Kaplan, H., & Roth, G. (2002). Choice is good, but relevance is excellent: Autonomy-enhancing and suppressing teacher behaviors predicting students' engagement in schoolwork. *British Journal of Educational Psychology, 72,* 261–278.

Atwood, G., & Karunannithi, S. (2002). Diversification of synaptic strength: Presynaptic elements. *Nature Reviews Neuroscience, 3,* 497–515.

Balter, M. (2000). Was Lamarck just a little bit right? *Science, 288,* 39.

Barron, B. (2000). Problem solving in video-based microworlds: Collaborative and individual outcomes of high-achieving sixth-grade students. *Journal of Educational Psychology, 92,* 391–398.

Barth, J., Dunlap, S., Dane, H., Lochman, J., & Wells, K. (2004). Classroom environment influences on aggression, peer relations, and academic focus. *Journal of School Psychology, 42,* 115–133.

Bechara, A., Damasio, H., & Damasio, A. (2003). Role of the amygdala in decision-making. *Annals of the New York Academy of Sciences, 985,* 356–369.

Betts, J. R., & Morell, D. (1999). The determinants of undergraduate grade point average: The relative importance of family background, high school resources, and peer group effects. *Journal of Human Resources, 34,* 268–293.

Bielaczyc, K., Pirolli, P., & Brown, A. L. (1995). Training in self-explanation and self-regulation strategies: Investigating the effects of knowledge acquisition activities on problem solving. *Cognition and Instruction, 13,* 221–252.

Blissitt, P. A. (2001). Sleep, memory, and learning. *Journal of Neuroscience Nursing, 33*(4), 208–215.

Bobby, Z., Koner, B., Sen, S., Renuka, P., Nandakumar, D., Nandeesha, H., et al. (2004). Small group discussion followed by presentation as a revision exercise at the end of a teaching module in biochemistry. *National Medical Journal of India, 17*(1), 36–38.

Boscolo, P., & Mason, L. (2000, April). *Prior knowledge, text coherence, and interest: How they interact in learning from instructional texts.* Paper presented at the Annual Meeting of the American Educational Research Association, New Orleans, LA.

Bouffard, T., Marcoux, M. F., Vezeau, C., & Bordeleau, L. (2003). Changes in self-perceptions of competence and intrinsic motivation among elementary schoolchildren. *British Journal of Educational Psychology, 73*, 171–186.

Bower, B. (1987). Memory boost from spaced-out learning. *Science News, 131*, 244.

Brigham, F. J., & Scruggs, T. E. (1995). Elaborative maps for enhanced learning of historical information: Uniting spatial, verbal, and imaginal information. *Journal of Special Education, 28*, 440–460.

Bryson, K. (1996). *Household and family characteristics: March 1995* (Current Population Reports, Series P20-488). Washington, DC: U.S. Government Printing Office. Retrieved March 7, 2008, from http://www.census.gov/prod/2/pop/p20/p20-488.pdf

Butler, A., Phillmann, K. B., & Smart, L. (2001). Active learning within a lecture: Assessing the impact of short, in-class writing exercises. *Teaching of Psychology, 28*, 257–259.

Cacioppo, J., Berntson, G., Sheridan, J., & McClintock, M. (2001). Multilevel analyses of human behavior: Social neuroscience and the complementing nature of social and biological approaches. In J. Cacioppo et al. (Eds.), *Foundations of social neuroscience* (pp. 21–46). Cambridge, MA: MIT Press.

Cairns, J., Overbaugh, J., & Miller, S. (1988). The origin of mutants. *Nature, 335*, 142–145.

Callicott, J. H., Mattay, V. S., Bertolino, A., Finn, K., Coppola, R., Frank, J. A., et al. (1999). Physiological characteristics of capacity constraints in working memory as revealed by functional MRI. *Cerebral Cortex, 9*, 20–26.

Carlson, R., Chandler, P., & Sweller, J. (2003). Learning and understanding science instructional material. *Journal of Educational Psychology, 95*, 629–640.

Carr, S. C., & Thompson, B. (1996). The effects of prior knowledge and schema activation strategies on the inferential reading comprehension of children with and without learning disabilities. *Learning Disability Quarterly, 19*, 48–61.

Carter, C., MacDonald, A., & Ursu, S. (2000, November). Based on findings presented at the 30th Annual Meeting of the Society for Neuroscience, New Orleans, LA.

Carver, S. (2001). Cognition and instruction: Enriching the laboratory school experience of children, teachers, parents, and undergraduates. In S. Carver & D. Klahr (Eds.), *Cognition and instruction: Twenty-five years of progress* (pp. 385–426). Mahwah, NJ: Lawrence Erlbaum.

Case, A., & Katz, L. (1991). *The company you keep: The effect of family and neighborhood on disadvantaged youths* (National Bureau of Economic Research Working Paper 3705). Cambridge, MA: National Bureau of Economic Research.

Cave, B. (1997). Very long-lasting priming in picture naming. *Psychological Science, 8*, 322–325.

Centers for Disease Control and Prevention. (2002). *2001 national school-based youth risk behavior survey.* Washington, DC: Author. Retrieved March 7, 2008, from http://www.cdc.gov/HealthyYouth/yrbs/data/2001/yrbs2001.pdf

Chaouloff, F. (1989). Physical exercise and brain monoamines: A review. *Acta Physiologica Scandinavica, 137,* 1–13.

Character Education Partnership. (2005). *Classroom-school climate* Retrieved April 11, 2008, from http://www.character.org/site/c.gwKUJhNYJrF/b.995169/k.5B53/ClassroomSchool_Climate.htm

Chen, H., & Lan, W. (1998). Adolescents' perceptions of their parents' academic expectations: Comparison of American, Chinese-American, and Chinese high school students. *Adolescence, 33,* 385–390.

Chesebro, J. (2003). Effects of teacher clarity and nonverbal immediacy on student learning, receiver apprehension, and affect. *Communication Education, 52,* 135–147.

Christen, W. L., & Murphy, T. J. (1991). Increasing comprehension by activating prior knowledge. *ERIC Digest.* Retrieved April 9, 2008, from http://www.ericdigests.org/pre-9219/prior.htm

Clarke, H. F., Dalley, J. W., Crofts, H. S., Robbins, T. W., & Roberts, A. C. (2004). Cognitive inflexibility after prefrontal serotonin depletion. *Science, 304,* 878–880.

Coleman, E., Rivkin, I., & Brown, A. (1997). The effect of instructional explanations on learning from scientific texts. *Journal of the Learning Sciences, 6,* 347–365.

Colicos, M., & Goda, Y. (2001). Pictures reveal how nerve cells form connections to store short- and long-term memories in brain. *Cell, 107,* 605–616.

Collie, A., Maruff, P., Darby, D. G., & McStephen, M. (2003). The effects of practice on the cognitive test performance of neurologically normal individuals assessed at brief test-retest intervals. *Journal of the International Neuropsychology Society, 9,* 419–428.

Cowan, N. (2001). The magical number 4 in short-term memory: A reconsideration of mental storage capacity. *Behavioral and Brain Sciences, 24,* 87–114.

Dahl, R. E. (1999). The consequences of insufficient sleep for adolescents. *Phi Delta Kappan, 80,* 354.

D'Alessandra, A., & Devyani Sadha1, D. (1998). The dimensions and measurement of school culture: Understanding school culture as the basis for school reform. *International Journal of Educational Research, 27,* 553–569.

Davies, S. (1999). Subcultural explanations and interpretations of school deviance. *Aggression and Violent Behavior, 4,* 191–202.

Deci, E. L., & Ryan, R. M. (2002). The paradox of achievement: The harder you push, the worse it gets. In J. Aronson (Ed.), *Improving academic achievement: Impact of psychological factors on education* (pp. 62–90). New York: Academic Press.

Dee, T. (2004). The race connection. *Education Next, 4*(2), 53–59.

Deutschman, C. S. (2005). Transcription. *Critical Care Medicine, 33*(Suppl.), S400–S403.

Di Vesta, F. J., & Smith, D. A. (1979). The pausing principle: Increasing the efficiency of memory for ongoing events. *Contemporary Educational Psychology, 4,* 288–296.

DiSessa, A. (1986). Models of computation. In D. A. Norman & S. W. Draper (Eds.), *User-centered system design: New perspectives in human-computer interaction* (pp. 201–218). Hillsdale, NJ: Lawrence Erlbaum.

Dochy, F., Segers, M., & Buehl, M. (1999). The relationship between assessment practices and outcomes of studies: The case of research on prior knowledge. *Review of Educational Research, 69,* 145–186.

Dudai, Y. (2004). The neurobiology of consolidations, or, how stable is the engram? *Annual Review of Psychology, 55,* 51–86.

Duyme, M., Dumaret, A.C., & Tomkiewicz, S. (1999). How can we boost IQs of "dull children"? A late adoption study. *Proceedings of the National Academy of Sciences of the United States of America, 96,* 8790–8794.

Eichenbaum, H. (2004). Hippocampus: Cognitive processes and neural representations that underlie declarative memory. *Neuron, 44,* 109–120.

Eisenberger, N. I., Jarcho, J. M., Lieberman, M. D., & Naliboff, B. D. (2006). An experimental study of shared sensitivity to physical pain and social rejection. *Pain, 126,* 132–138.

Environmental Protection Agency. (2000). *Indoor air quality and student performance* (EPA report number EPA 402-F-00-009). Washington, DC: Author. Retrieved April 11, 2008, from http://www.eric.ed.gov/contentdelivery/servlet/ERICServlet?accno=%20ED453639

Ericsson, K. A. (1996). The acquisition of expert performance. In K. A. Ericsson (Ed.), *The road to excellence: The acquisition of expert performance in the arts, science, and games* (pp. 1–50). Mahwah, NJ: Lawrence Erlbaum.

Evans, G. W., & Maxwell, L. (1999). Chronic noise exposure and reading deficits: The mediating effects of language acquisition. *Environment and Behavior, 29,* 638–656.

Eysenck, M. W., & Eysenck, M. C. (1979). Processing depth, elaboration of encoding, memory stores, and expended processing capacity. *Journal of Experimental Psychology: Human Learning and Memory, 5,* 472–484.

Farragher, P., & Yore, L. D. (1997). The effects of embedded monitoring and regulating devices on the achievement of high school students learning science from text. *School Science and Mathematics, 97,* 87–95.

Feth, L. (1999, December 24). Many classrooms have bad acoustics that inhibit learning. *ScienceDaily.* Retrieved April 11, 2008, from http://www.sciencedaily.com/releases/1999/12/991224090246.htm

Fiore, S., Cuevas, D., Haydee, M., & Oser, R. (2003). A picture is worth a thousand connections: The facilitative effects of diagrams on mental model development and task performance. *Computers in Human Behavior, 19,* 185–199.

Fischer, K. W. (2000). From individual differences to dynamic pathways of development. *Child Development. Jul-Aug; 71*(4): 850–3.

Frank, L., Stanley, G., & Brown, E. (2004). Hippocampal plasticity across multiple days of exposure to novel environments. *Journal of Neuroscience, 24,* 7681–7689.

Furneaux, C. (2002). Teaching writing using peer feedback checklists. *ESL Magazine, 5*(3), 16–18.

Furrer, C., & Skinner, E. (2003). Sense of relatedness as a factor in children's academic engagement and performance. *Journal of Educational Psychology, 95,* 148–162.

Futrell, M., Gomez, J., & Bedden, D. (2003). Teaching the children of a new America. *Phi Delta Kappan, 84,* 381–385.

Gellevij, M., Van der Meij, H., deJong, T., & Pieters, J. (2002). Multimodal versus unimodal instruction in a complex learning context. *Journal of Experimental Education, 70,* 215–39.

Gentner, D., & Stevens, A. (1983). *Mental models.* Hillsdale, NJ: Lawrence Erlbaum.

Ghaith, G. M. (2002). The relationship between cooperative learning, perception of social support, and academic achievement. *System, 30,* 263–273.

Gifford-Smith, M., & Brownell, C. (2003). Childhood peer relationships: Social acceptance, friendships, and peer networks. *Journal of School Psychology, 41,* 235–284.

Gillberg, M., Anderzen, I., Akerstedt, T., & Sigurdson, K. (1986). Urinary catecholamine responses to basic types of physical activity. *European Journal of Applied Physiology, 55,* 575–578.

Gillies, R., & Ashman, A. (1998). Behavior and interactions of children in cooperative groups in lower and middle elementary grades. *Journal of Educational Psychology, 90,* 1–12.

Gomez-Pinilla, F., So, V., & Kesslak, J. (1998). Spatial learning and physical activity contribute to the induction of fibroblast growth factor: Neural substrates for increased cognition associated with exercise. *Neuroscience, 85,* 53–61.

Gooda, C., Aronson, J., & Inzlicht, M. (2003). Improving adolescents' standardized test performance: An intervention to reduce the effects of stereotype threat. *Journal of Applied Developmental Psychology, 24,* 645–662.

Goodman, J. S., Wood, R. E., & Hendrickx, M. (2004). Feedback specificity, exploration, and learning. *Journal of Applied Psychology, 89,* 248–262.

Gratton, G., Bosco, C., Kramer, A., Coles, M., Wickens, C., & Donchin, E. (1992). Event-related brain potentials as indices of information extraction and response priming. *Journal of Experimental Psychology: General, 121,* 480–506.

Gratton, G., Coles, M. G., & Donchin, E. (2002). Optimizing the use of information: Strategic control of activation of responses. *Cognition, 85*(2), B43–50.

Gray, J., Braver, T., & Raichle, M. (2002). Integration of emotion and cognition in the lateral prefrontal cortex. *Proceedings of the National Academy of Sciences of the United States of America, 99,* 4115–4120.

Greenberg, M., Weissberg, R., O'Brien, M., Zinsa, J., Fredericks, L., Resnik, H., et al. (2003). Enhancing school-based prevention and youth development through coordinated social, emotional, and academic learning. *American Psychologist, 58,* 466–474.

Gregoire, M., Ashton, P., & Algina, J. (2004). Authoritative schools: A test of a model to resolve the school effectiveness debate. *Contemporary Educational Psychology, 29,* 389–409.

Hagmann, M. (1999). How chromatin changes its shape. *Science, 285,* 1200–1201, 1203.

Haier, R. J., Siegel, B. V., Jr., MacLachlan, A., Soderling, E., Lottenberg, S., & Buchsbaum, M. S. (1992). Regional glucose metabolic changes after learning a complex visuospatial/motor task: A positron emission tomographic study. *Brain Research, 570*(1–2), 134–143.

Hambrick, D. Z. (2003). Why are some people more knowledgeable than others? A longitudinal study of knowledge acquisition. *Memory & Cognition, 31,* 902–917.

Harlow, H., & Harlow, M. (1973). Social deprivation in monkeys. In *Readings from Scientific American: The nature and nurture of behavior* (pp. 108–116). San Francisco: W. H. Freeman.

Harris, J. (1998). *The nurture assumption: Why children turn out the way they do.* New York: Free Press.

Hathaway, W. (1992). *A study into the effects of types of light on children: A case of daylight robbery* (IRC Internal Report No. 659). Edmonton, Canada: Hathaway Planning & Consulting Services.

Hattie, J., Biggs, J., & Purdie, N. (1996). Effects of learning skills interventions on student learning: A meta-analysis. *Review of Educational Research, 66,* 99–136.

Hayes, B. K., Foster, K., & Gadd, N. (2003). Prior knowledge and subtyping effects in children's category learning. *Cognition, 88,* 177–199.

Heindel, J., McAllister, K., Worth, L., Jr., & Tyson, F. L. (2006). Environmental epigenomics, imprinting and disease susceptibility. *Epigenetics, 1,* 1–6.

Heschong Mahone Group. (1999). [Daylighting in schools: An investigation into the relationship between daylighting and human performance]. Unpublished data.

Heschong Mahone Group. (2008). *Windows and classrooms: A study of student performance and the indoor environment—CEC Pier 2003.* Retrieved March 7, 2008, from http://www.h-m-g.com/projects/daylighting/summaries%20on%20daylighting.htm

Hirschy, A. S., & Wilson, M. E. (2002). The sociology of the classroom and its influence on student learning. *Peabody Journal of Education, 77*(3), 85–100.

Hopf, F., Waters, J., Mehta, S., & Smith, S. (2002). Stability and plasticity of developing synapses in hippocampal neuronal cultures. *Journal of Neuroscience, 22,* 775–781.

House, J., Landis, K., & Umberson, D. (1988). Social relationships and health. *Science, 241,* 540–545.

Huang, S. (2000). A quantitative analysis of audiotaped and written feedback produced for students' writing and students' perceptions of the two feedback methods. *Tunghai Journal, 4,* 199–232.

Huang, S. C., Tsai, S. J., & Chang, J. C. (2004). Fluoxetine-induced memory impairment in four family members. *International Journal of Psychiatry in Medicine, 34,* 197–200.

Huttenlocher, P. (2002). *Neural plasticity.* Cambridge, MA: Harvard University Press.

Hyerle, D. (2004). *Student successes with thinking maps.* Thousand Oaks, CA: Corwin Press.

Hyland, F. (1998). The impact of teacher written feedback on individual writers. *Journal of Second Language Writing, 7,* 255–286.

Jacobs, B., Schall, M., & Scheibel, A. (1993). A quantitative dendritic analysis of Wernicke's area in humans. II. Gender, hemispheric, and environmental factors. *Journal of Comparative Neurology, 327,* 97–111.

Jensen. (2006). *Enriching the brain.* San Francisco: Jossey-Bass.

Johnson, D., & Johnson, R. (1999). *Learning together and alone: Cooperative, competitive and individualistic learning.* Boston: Allyn & Bacon.

Johnson-Laird, P. (1983). *Mental models: Towards a cognitive science of language, inference, and consciousness.* Cambridge, MA: Harvard University Press.

Jonsdottir, V., Laukkanen, A. M., & Siikki, I. (2003). Changes in teachers' voice quality during a working day with and without electric sound amplification. *Folia Phoniatrica et Logopaedica, 55,* 267–280.

Joussemet, M., Koestner, R., Lekes, N., & Houlfort, N. (2004). Introducing uninteresting tasks to children: A comparison of the effects of rewards and autonomy support. *Journal of Personality, 72,* 139–166.

Kandel, E. R. (1998). A new intellectual framework for psychiatry. *American Journal of Psychiatry, 155,* 457–469.

Kann, L., Kinchen, S., Williams, B., Ross, J., Lowry, R., Grunbaum, J., et al. (2000). Youth risk behavior surveillance—United States, 1999. *Morbidity and Mortality Weekly Report, 49*(SS-5). Retrieved April 14, 2008, from http://www.cdc.gov/mmwr/PDF/ss/ss4905.pdf

Kaplan, A. S., & Murphy, G. L. (2000). Category learning with minimal prior knowledge. *Journal of Experimental Psychology: Learning, Memory, Cognition, 26,* 829–846.

Kenny, M., Blustein, D., Chaves, A., Grossman, J., & Gallagher, L. (2003). The role of perceived barriers and relational support in the educational and vocational lives of urban high school students. *Journal of Counseling Psychology, 50,* 142–155.

Kiewra, K. A. (1985). More notes were better than less: Providing the instructor's notes: An effective addition to student notetaking. *Educational Psychologist, 20,* 33–39.

Kilgard, M. P., & Merzenich, M. M. (1998). Cortical map reorganization enabled by nucleus basalis activity. *Science, 279,* 1714–1718.

Kilgard, M., & Merzenich, M. (2002). Order-sensitive plasticity in adult primary auditory cortex. *Proceedings of the National Academy of Sciences of the United States of America, 99,* 3205–3209.

Kim J., & Diamond, D. (2002). The stressed hippocampus, synaptic plasticity and lost memories. *Nature Reviews Neuroscience, 3,* 453–462.

Kirkland, C. (1995). *Using advance organizers with learning disabled students.* Paper presented at the Annual Meeting of the American Educational Research Association, San Francisco. (ERIC Document Reproduction Service No. ED390379)

Klingberg, T. (2000). Limitations in information processing in the human brain: Neuroimaging of dual task performance and working memory tasks. *Progress in Brain Research, 126,* 95–102.

Kluger, A., & DeNisi, A. (1996). The effects of feedback interventions on performance: A historical review, a meta-analysis, and a preliminary feedback intervention theory. *Psychological Bulletin, 119,* 254–284.

Krock, L. P., & Hartung, G. H. (1992). Influence of post-exercise activity on plasma catecholamines, blood pressure and heart rate in normal subjects. *Clinical Autonomic Research, 2*(2), 89–97.

Lachter, J., & Hayhoe, M. (1995). Capacity limitations in memory for visual locations. *Perception, 24,* 1427–1441.

Lackney, J. (1994). *Educational facilities: The impact and role of the physical environment of the school on teaching, learning and educational outcomes: Multi-disciplinary model for assessing impact of infrastructure on education and student achievement using applied research.* Milwaukee: University of Wisconsin-Milwaukee, Center for Architecture and Urban Planning Research.

Latham, A. S. (1997). Learning through feedback. *Educational Leadership, 54*(8), 86–87.

Lee, D. D., & Francis, M. (1994). The effect of varied feedback strategies on students' cognitive and attitude development. *International Journal of Instructional Media, 21*(1), 13–21.

Lehman, S., & Schraw, G. (2002). Effects of coherence and relevance on shallow and deep text processing. *Journal of Educational Psychology, 94,* 738–750.

Lemasters, L. (1997). *A synthesis of studies pertaining to facilities, student achievement, and student behavior.* Blacksburg: Virginia Polytechnic and State University. (ERIC Document Reproduction Service No. ED447687)

Levin, J. R. (1988). Elaboration-based learning strategies: Powerful theory = powerful application. *Contemporary Educational Psychology, 13,* 191–205.

Lipsey, M., & Wilson, D. (1993). The efficacy of psychological, educational and behavioral treatment. *American Psychologist, 48,* 1181–1209.

Lipton, B. (2005). *The biology of belief: Unleashing the power of consciousness, matter, and miracles.* Santa Clara, CA: Mountain of Love/Elite Books.

Manuck, S. B., Flory, J. D., Ferrell, R. E., & Muldoon, M. F. (2004). Socio-economic status covaries with central nervous system serotonergic responsivity as a function of allelic variation in the serotonin transporter gene-linked polymorphic region. *Psychoneuroendocrinology, 29,* 651–668.

Maquet, P., Peigneux, P., Laureys, S., & Smith, C. (2002). Be caught napping: You're doing more than resting your eyes. *Nature Neuroscience, 5,* 618–619.

Marjoribanks, R. (2003). Family and ability correlates of academic achievement: Social status group differences. *Psychological Reports, 93,* 419–422.

Martin, A., & Turennout, M. (2002). Searching for the neural correlates of object priming. In D. Schacter & L. Squire (Eds.), *Neuropsychology of memory* (pp. 239–247). New York: Guilford Press.

Marzano, R., Kendall, J., & Gaddy, B. (1999). *Essential knowledge: The debate over what American students should know.* Aurora, CO: Mid-continent Research in Education and Learning.

Matthews, G., Campbell, S., Falconer, S., Joyner, L., Huggins, J., Gilliland, K., et al. (2002). Fundamental dimensions of subjective state in performance settings: Task engagement, distress, and worry. *Emotion, 2,* 315–340.

McCarthy, M. T. (1995). Form of feedback effects on verb learning and near-transfer tasks by sixth graders. *Contemporary Educational Psychology, 20,* 140–150.

McCraty, R., Atkinson, M., Tomasino, D., Goelitz, J., & Mayrovitz, H. N. (1999). The impact of an emotional self-management skills course on psychosocial functioning and autonomic recovery to stress in middle school children. *Integrative Physiological and Behavioral Science, 34,* 246–268.

McGee, Z., Davis, B., Brisbane, T., Collins, N., Nuriddin, T., Irving, S., et al. (2001). Urban stress and mental health among African-American youth: Assessing the link between exposure to violence, problem behavior, and coping strategies. *Journal of Cultural Diversity, 8*(3), 94–104.

McLachlan, J. (2003). Using models to enhance the intellectual content of learning in developmental biology. *International Journal of Developmental Biology, 47,* 225–229.

McNamara, D. S. (2001). Reading both high-coherence and low-coherence texts: Effects of text sequence and prior knowledge. *Canadian Journal of Experimental Psychology, 55,* 51–62.

McNamara, D., & Kintsch, W. (1996). Learning from texts: Effects of prior knowledge and text coherence. *Discourse Processes, 22,* 247–288.

McNamara, D., & McDaniel, M. (2004). Suppressing irrelevant information: Knowledge activation or inhibition? *Journal of Experimental Psychology: Learning, Memory, and Cognition, 30,* 465–482.

Mednick, S. C., Nakayama, K., Cantero, J. L., Atienza, M., Levin, A. A., Pathak, N., et al. (2002). The restorative effect of naps on perceptual deterioration. *Nature Neuroscience, 5,* 677–681.

Mednick, S., Nakayama, K., & Stickgold, R. (2003). Sleep-dependent learning: A nap is as good as a night. *Nature Neuroscience, 6,* 697–698.

Mendel, L. L., Roberts, R. A., & Walton, J. H. (2003). Speech perception benefits from sound field FM amplification. *American Journal of Audiology, 12,* 114–124.

Mendes, E. (2002). *The relationship between emotional intelligence and occupational burnout in secondary school teachers.* Ann Arbor, MI: ProQuest Information and Learning.

Moore, G., & Lackney, J. (1993). School design. *Children's Environments, 10,* 99–112.

Motl, R., Birnbaum, A., Kubik, M., & Dishman, R. (2004). Naturally occurring changes in physical activity are inversely related to depressive symptoms during early adolescence. *Psychosomatic Medicine, 66,* 336–342.

Moulaert, V., Verwijnen, M., Rikers, R., & Scherpbier, A. (2004). The effects of deliberate practice in undergraduate medical education. *Medical Education, 38,* 1044–1052.

Mueller, C., & Dweck, C. (1998). Praise for intelligence can undermine children's motivation and performance. *Journal of Personality and Social Psychology, 75,* 33–52.

Nadel, L., & Land, C. (2000). Memory traces revisited. *Nature Reviews Neuroscience, 1,* 209–12.

Najaka, S. S., Gottfredson, D. C., & Wilson, D. B. (2001). A meta-analytic inquiry into the relationship between selected risk factors and problem behavior. *Prevention Science, 2,* 257–271.

National Center for Education Statistics. (2003). *Indicators of school crime and safety.* Retrieved April 11, 2008, from http://nces.ed.gov/pubs2004/crime03/

Nelson, P., & Soli, S. (2000). Acoustical barriers to learning: Children at risk in every classroom. *Language, Speech & Hearing Services in Schools, 4,* 356–361.

Newcomer, J. W., Selke, G., Melson, A. K., Hershey, T., Craft, S., Richards, K., et al. (1999). Decreased memory performance in healthy humans induced by stress-level cortisol treatment. *Archives of General Psychiatry, 56,* 527–533.

Newman, R. (2000). Social influences on the development of children's adaptive help seeking: The role of parents, teachers, and peers. *Developmental Review, 20,* 350–404.

Nitko, A. (2001). *Educational assessment of students.* Upper Saddle River, NJ: Prentice Hall.

Nuthall, G. (1999). The way students learn: Acquiring knowledge from an integrated science and social studies unit. *Elementary School Journal, 99,* 303–341.

Nuthall, G., & Alton-Lee, A. (1995). Assessing classroom learning: How students use their knowledge and experience to answer classroom achievement test questions in science and social studies. *American Educational Research Journal, 32,* 185–223.

Ochsner, K. N., Chiu, C.-Y. P., & Schacter, D. L. (1998). Varieties of priming. In L. Squire & S. Kosslyn (Eds.), *Findings and current opinion in cognitive neuroscience* (pp. 99–104). Cambridge, MA: MIT Press.

O'Neil, R., Welsh, M., Parke, R. D., Wang, S., & Strand, C. (1997). A longitudinal assessment of the academic correlates of early peer acceptance and rejection. *Journal of Clinical Child Psychology, 26,* 290–303.

Onwuegbuzie, A. J., Slate, J. R., Paterson, F. R. A., Watson, M. H., & Schwartz, R. A. (2000). Factors associated with achievement in educational research courses. *Research in the Schools, 7*(1), 53–65.

Ozer, E. M., Park, M. J., Paul, T., Brindis, C. D., & Irwin, C. E., Jr. (2003). *America's adolescents: Are they healthy?* San Francisco: University of California, National Adolescent Health Information Center. Retrieved March 7, 2008, from http://nahic.ucsf.edu/download.php?f=/downloads/AA_2003.pdf

Padgett, D., & Sheridan, J. (1999). *Social stress, dominance and increased mortality from an influenza viral infection.* Manuscript submitted for publication.

Padgett, D., Sheridan, J., Dorne, J., Berntson, G., Candelora, J., & Glaser, R. (1998). Social stress and the reactivation of latent herpes simplex virus type I.

Proceedings of the National Academy of Sciences of the United States of America, 95, 7231–7235.

Palincsar, A. S., & Brown, A. L. (1984). Reciprocal teaching in comprehension-fostering and comprehension-monitoring activities. *Cognition and Instruction, 1*(2), 117–175.

Panksepp, J. (2003). Feeling the pain of social loss. *Science, 302,* 237–239.

Parker, W. (2005). Teaching against idiocy. *Phi Delta Kappan, 86,* 344–351.

Peeck, J., van den Bosch, A. B., & Kreupeling, W. J. (1985). Effects of informative feedback in relation to retention of initial responses. *Contemporary Educational Psychology, 10,* 303–313.

Peeters, G., & Czapinski, J. (1990). Positive-negative asymmetry in evaluations: The distinction between affective and informational negativity effects. In W. Stroebe & M. Hewstone (Eds.), *European review of social psychology* (Vol. 1, pp. 33–60). Chichester, England: Wiley & Sons.

Pekkarinen, E., & Wiljanen, V. (1990). Effect of sound-absorbing treatment on speech discrimination in rooms. *Audiology, 29,* 219–227.

Penner, D., Giles, N., Lehrer, R., & Schauble, L. (1997). Building functional models: Designing an elbow. *Journal of Research in Science Teaching, 34,* 125–143.

Phillips, N. B., Fuchs, L. S., & Fuchs, D. (1994). Effects of classwide curriculum-based measurement and peer tutoring: A collaborative researcher–practitioner interview study. *Journal of Learning Disabilities, 27,* 420–434.

Phye, G. D., & Sanders, C. E. (1994). Advice and feedback: Elements of practice for problem solving. *Contemporary Educational Psychology, 19,* 286–301.

Power, F. C., Higgins, A., & Kohlberg, L. (1989). *Approach to moral education.* New York: Columbia University Press.

Reynolds, D., Nicolson, R., & Hambly, H. (2003). Evaluation of an exercise-based treatment for children with reading difficulties. *Dyslexia, 9,* 48–71.

Riccomini, P. (2002). The comparative effectiveness of two forms of feedback: Web-based model comparison and instructor delivered corrective feedback. *Journal of Educational Computing Research, 27,* 213–228.

Richard, A. (2004, May 12). Stuck in time. *Education Week,* p. 15.

Roozendaal, B. (2002). Stress and memory: Opposing effects of glucocorticoids on memory consolidation and memory retrieval. *Neurobiology of Learning and Memory, 78,* 578–595.

Rosenthal, R. (1991). Teacher expectancy effects: A brief update 25 years after the Pygmalion experiment. *Journal of Research in Education, 1,* 3–12.

Rosenthal, R., & Jacobson, L. (1996). Teachers' expectancies: Determinants of pupils' IQ gains. *Psychological Reports, 19,* 115–118.

Rossi, E. (2002). *The psychobiology of gene expression: Neuroscience and neurogenesis in therapeutic hypnosis and the healing arts.* New York: Norton Professional Books.

Ruhl, K., Hughes, C., & Schloss, P. (1987). Using the pause procedure to enhance lecture recall. *Teacher Education and Special Education, 10,* 14–18.

Ruscio, J. (2001). Administering quizzes at random to increase students' reading. *Teaching of Psychology, 28,* 204–206.

Russell, I. J., Hendricson, W. D., & Herbert, R. J. (1984). Effects of lecture information density on medical student achievement. *Journal of Medical Education, 59,* 881–889.

Ryan, R., & Deci, E. (2000). Self-determination theory and the facilitation of intrinsic motivation, social development, and well-being. *American Psychologist, 55,* 68–78.

Sadoski, M., Goetz, E., & Joyce, F. (1993). Impact of concreteness on comprehensibility, interest, and memory for text: Implications for dual coding theory and text design. *Journal of Educational Psychology, 85,* 291–304.

Schacter, D. L. (2001). *The seven sins of memory.* New York: Houghton Mifflin.

Schneider, M. (2002). *Do school facilities affect academic outcomes?* Washington, DC: National Clearinghouse for Educational Facilities.

Schroth, M. L. (1997). Effects of frequency of feedback on transfer in concept identification. *American Journal of Psychology, 110,* 71–79.

Schulla-Cose, D., & Day, K. (2004). Shaping a school culture. *Educational Leadership, 61*(4), 88–89.

Schwartz, P., Rosenthal, N., & Wehr, T. (1998). Serotonin 1A receptors, melatonin, and the proportional control thermostat in patients with winter depression. *Archives of Psychiatry, 55,* 897–903.

Seligman, M. (2006). *Learned optimism: How to change your mind and your life.* New York: Pocket Books.

Sforzo, G. A., Seeger, T. F., Pert, C. B., Pert, A., & Dotson, C. O. (1986). In vivo opioid receptor occupation in the rat brain following exercise. *Medicine and Science in Sports and Exercise, 18,* 380–384.

Shadmehr, R., & Holcomb, H. H. (1997). Neural correlates of motor memory consolidation. *Science, 277,* 821–825.

Simpson, J., Jr., Snyder, A., Gusnard, D., & Raichle, M. (2000). Emotion-induced changes in human medial prefrontal cortex during cognitive task performance. *Proceedings of the National Academy of Sciences of the United States of America, 98,* 683–687.

Slavin, R. (1994). Quality, appropriateness, incentive, and time: A model of instructional effectiveness. *International Journal of Educational Research, 21,* 141–157.

Smaldino, J., & Crandell, C. (2000). Classroom amplification technology: Theory and practice. *Language, Speech & Hearing Services in Schools, 4,* 371–375.

Smith, A. (2003). Peer relationships in physical activity contexts: A road less traveled in youth sport and exercise psychology research. *Psychology of Sport and Exercise, 4,* 25–39.

Smith, E., Walker, K., Fields, L., Brookins, C., & Seay, R. (1999). Ethnic identity and its relationship to self-esteem, perceived efficacy and prosocial attitudes. *Early Adolescence Journal of Adolescence, 22,* 867–880.

Snyder, C., Shorey, H., Cheavens, J., Pulvers, K., Adams, V., & Wiklund, C. (2002). Hope and academic success in college. *Journal of Educational Psychology, 94,* 820–826.

Snyder, S. (1991, April). *The effect of instructional clarity and concept structure on student achievement and perception.* Paper presented at the Annual Meeting of the American Educational Research Association, Chicago.

Snyder, S. (1993, April). *Instructional clarity: The role of linking and focusing moves on student achievement, motivation, and satisfaction.* Paper presented at the Annual Meeting of the American Educational Research Association, Atlanta, GA.

Soler, E. (2003). Relationship between teacher-led versus learners' interaction and the development of pragmatics in the EFL classroom. *International Journal of Educational Research, 37,* 359–377.

Southern Poverty Law Center. (n.d.). *101 tools for tolerance.* Retrieved April 11, 2008, from http://www.tolerance.org/101_tools/index.html

Spires, H. A., & Donley, J. (1998). Prior knowledge activation: Inducing engagement with informational texts. *Journal of Educational Psychology, 90,* 249–260.

Stahl, R. J. (1994). Using "think-time" and "wait-time" skillfully in the classroom. *ERIC Digest.* Retrieved April 14, 2008, from http://www.ericdigests.org/1995-1/think.htm

Steinberg, L., Dornbusch, S. M., & Brown, B. B. (1992). Ethnic differences in adolescent achievement: An ecological perspective. *American Psychologist, 47,* 723–729.

Sternberg, R. (2003). Our research program validating the triarchic theory of successful intelligence. *Intelligence, 31,* 399–413.

Sternberg, R., & Grigorenko, E. (Eds.). (2001). *Environmental effects on cognitive abilities.* New York: Basic Books.

Stickgold, R., Fosse, R., & Walker, M. (2002). Linking brain and behavior in sleep-dependent learning and memory consolidation. *Proceedings of the National Academy of Sciences of the United States of America, 99,* 16519–16521.

Stickgold, R., & Walker, M. (2004). To sleep, perchance to gain creative insight? *Trends in Cognitive Sciences, 8,* 191–192.

Sumby, W. H. (1965). Incremental or one-trial learning of verbal series. ESD-TR-64-555. Tech Doc Rep U. S. Air Force Syst Command Electron Syst. Div. (Oct: 1-18).

Summers, C. H., Forster, G. L., Korzan, W. J., Watt, M. J., Larson, E. T., Øverli, O., et al. (2004). Dynamics and mechanics of social rank reversal. *Journal of Comparative Physiology A: Neuroethology, Sensory, Neural, and Behavioral Physiology, 191,* 241–252.

Thorne, B. (2000). Extra credit exercise: A painless pop quiz. *Teaching of Psychology, 27,* 204–205.

Titsworth, B. S. (2001). The effects of teacher immediacy: Use of organizational lecture cues and students' notetaking on cognitive learning. *Communication Education, 50,* 283–297.

Tomporowski, P. (2003). Effects of acute bouts of exercise on cognition. *Acta Psychologica, 112,* 297–324.

Tucker, C., & Herman, K. (2002). Using culturally sensitive theories and research to meet the academic needs of low-income African American children. *American Psychologist, 57,* 762–773.

U.S. Census Bureau. (2007). *Children's living arrangements and characteristics: March 2002.* Retrieved March 7, 2008, from http://www.census.gov/population/www/socdemo/hh-fam.html

U.S. Department of Education, Office of the Under Secretary, Policy and Program Studies Service. (2004). *National assessment of vocational education: Final report to Congress.* Washington, DC: Author.

U.S. General Accounting Office. (1995). Retrieved April 12, 2007, from http://www.gpoaccess.gov/gaoreports/index.html

U.S. Surgeon General. (1999). *Mental health: A report of the surgeon general.* Rockville, MD: National Institute of Mental Health. Retrieved March 7, 2008, from http://www.surgeongeneral.gov/library/mentalhealth/

Valeski, T. N., & Stipek, D. J. (2001). Young children's feelings about school. *Child Development, 72,* 1198–1213.

van Honk, J., Tuiten, A., van den Hout, M., Koppeschaar, H., Thijssen, J., de Haan, E., et al. (2000). Conscious and preconscious selective attention to social threat: Different neuroendocrine response patterns. *Psychoneuroendocrinology, 25,* 577–591.

Walberg, H. (1999). Productive teaching. In H. C. Waxman & H. Walberg (Eds.), *New directions for teaching practice and research* (pp. 75–104). Berkeley, CA: McCutchen.

Wallace, D., Wandell, S., West, C., & Ware, A. (1998). The effect of knowledge maps that incorporate gestalt principles on learning. *Journal of Experimental Education, 67,* 5–16.

Wattenmaker, W. D. (1999). The influence of prior knowledge in intentional versus incidental concept learning. *Memory & Cognition, 27,* 658–698.

Wessler, S. (2004). It's hard to learn when you're scared. *Educational Leadership, 61*(1), 40–43.

Wiedenmayer, C. P. (2004). Adaptations or pathologies? Long-term changes in brain and behavior after a single exposure to severe threat. *Neuroscience and Biobehavioral Reviews, 28,* 1–12.

Williams, R. M., & Wessel, J. (2004). Reflective journal writing to obtain student feedback about their learning during the study of chronic musculoskeletal conditions. *Journal of Allied Health, 33,* 17–23.

Willoughby, T., Porter, L., Belsito, L., & Yearsley, T. (1999). Use of elaboration strategies by students in grades two, four, and six. *Elementary School Journal, 99,* 221–231.

Wilson, M. A. (2002). Hippocampal memory formation, plasticity, and the role of sleep. *Neurobiology of Learning and Memory, 78,* 565–569.

Wiltgen, B. J., Brown, R. A., Talton, L. E., & Silva, A. J. (2004). New circuits for old memories: The role of the neocortex in consolidation. *Neuron, 44,* 101–108.

Wolfson, A. R., & Carskadon, M. A. (2003). Understanding adolescents' sleep patterns and school performance: A critical appraisal. *Sleep Medicine Reviews, 7,* 491–506.

Wood, C. (2002). Changing the pace of school: Slowing down the day to improve the quality of learning. *Phi Delta Kappan, 83,* 545–550.

Wood, E. (1994). Enhancing adolescents' recall of factual content: The impact of provided versus self-generated elaborations. *Alberta Journal of Educational Research, 40,* 57–65.

Wood, S. L., & Lynch, J. G., Jr. (2002). Prior knowledge and complacency in new product learning. *Journal of Consumer Research, 29,* 416–427.

Yazzie-Mintz, E. (2007). *Voices of students on engagement: A report on the 2006 High School Survey of Student Engagement.* Bloomington: Indiana University, Center for Evaluation & Education Policy. Retrieved April 10, 2008, from http://ceep.indiana.edu/hssse/pdf/HSSSE_2006_Report.pdf

Zimmerman, B., & Kitsantas, A. (2002). Acquiring writing revision and self-regulatory skill through observation and emulation. *Journal of Educational Psychology, 94,* 660–668.

Zohar, A. D. A., & Vaaknin, E. (2001). Teachers' beliefs about low-achieving students and higher order thinking. *Teaching and Teacher Education, 17,* 469–485.

Index

CORWIN PRESS

The Corwin Press logo—a raven striding across an open book—represents the union of courage and learning. Corwin Press is committed to improving education for all learners by publishing books and other professional development resources for those serving the field of PreK–12 education. By providing practical, hands-on materials, Corwin Press continues to carry out the promise of its motto: **"Helping Educators Do Their Work Better."**